SUGAR

Edible

Series Editor: Andrew F. Smith

EDIBLE is a revolutionary new series of books dedicated to food and drink that explores the rich history of cuisine. Each book reveals the global history and culture of one type of food or beverage.

Already published

Apple Erika Janik *Barbecue* Jonathan Deutsch and Megan
J. Elias *Beef* Lorna Piatti-Farnell *Beer* Gavin D. Smith
Brandy Becky Sue Epstein *Bread* William Rubel
Cake Nicola Humble *Caviar* Nichola Fletcher *Champagne*
Becky Sue Epstein *Cheese* Andrew Dalby *Chocolate* Sarah
Moss and Alexander Badenoch *Cocktails* Joseph M. Carlin
Curry Colleen Taylor Sen *Dates* Nawal Nasrallah *Dumplings*
Barbara Gallani *Eggs* Diane Toops *Figs* David C. Sutton
Game Paula Young Lee *Gin* Lesley Jacobs Solmonson
Hamburger Andrew F. Smith *Herbs* Gary Allen
Hot Dog Bruce Kraig *Ice Cream* Laura B. Weiss
Lemon Toby Sonneman *Lobster* Elisabeth Townsend
Milk Hannah Velten *Mushroom* Cynthia D. Bertelsen
Nuts Ken Albala *Offal* Nina Edwards *Olive* Fabrizia Lanza
Oranges Clarissa Hyman *Pancake* Ken Albala
Pie Janet Clarkson *Pineapple* Kaori O' Connor
Pizza Carol Helstosky *Pork* Katharine M. Rogers
Potato Andrew F. Smith *Pudding* Jeri Quinzio *Rice* Renee
Marton *Rum* Richard Foss *Salmon* Nicolaas Mink *Sandwich*
Bee Wilson *Sauces* Maryann Tebben *Soup* Janet Clarkson
Spices Fred Czarra *Sugar* Andrew F. Smith *Tea* Helen Saberi
Tequila Ian Williams *Truffle* Zachary Nowak *Vodka* Patricia
Herlihy *Whiskey* Kevin R. Kosar *Wine* Marc Millon

Sugar

A Global History

Andrew F. Smith

REAKTION BOOKS

To Meghanne, Reilly, Ethan and Owen
– may you enjoy sweets in moderation

Published by Reaktion Books Ltd
33 Great Sutton Street
London EC1V 0DX, UK
www.reaktionbooks.co.uk

First published 2015

Copyright © Andrew F. Smith 2015

Printed and bound in China

A catalogue record for this book is available
from the British Library

ISBN 978 1 78023 434 2

Contents

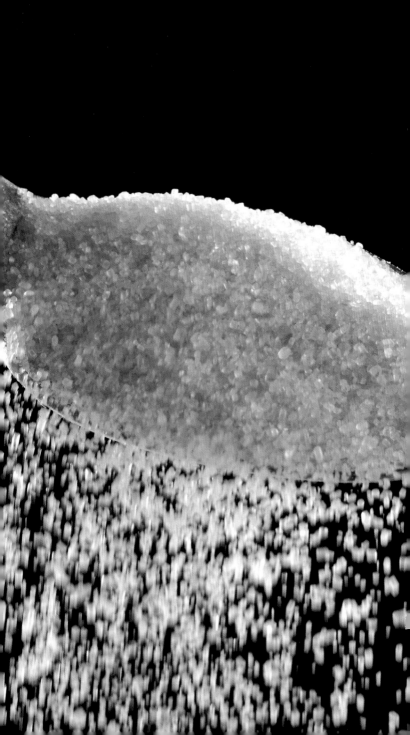

Prologue

From birth, humans are attracted to sweet-tasting foods, and for good reason: all 10,000 taste buds in the mouth have special receptors for sweetness. Sweet foods cause the taste buds to release neurotransmitters that light up the brain's pleasure centres. The brain responds by producing endo-cannabinoids, which increase appetite. This may have an evolutionary explanation: about 40 per cent of the calories in breast milk come from lactose, a disaccharide sugar that is readily metabolized into glucose, the body's basic fuel. The sweetness leads infants to eat more, making them more likely to survive.

Naturally bitter plants may signal toxicity, while sweet foods are generally safe to eat and are usually good sources of simple carbohydrates. Once we become conditioned to consume sweet foods, even the sight of them will cause us to salivate; the saliva will help begin the process of breaking down the carbohydrates, signalling to the digestive system that nutrients are on the way.

For millennia, our ancestors cultivated and bred sweet fruits and vegetables and sweetened foods with juice from fruit, berries, figs, dates, nuts and carrots, saps from carob, maple or palm trees, nectar from flowers, and the leaves and seeds of sweet herbs. Over the centuries humans have learned to harvest, refine or concentrate sweeteners such as maltose from grains, glucose from grapes, fructose from fruits, berries and corn, and sucrose from sugar cane and sugar beet. Humans have even harnessed the bee to provide honey, the Old World's first important sweetener.

The most common sweetener for the past 500 years, however, has been table sugar, or sucrose ($C_{12}H_{22}O_{11}$), a disaccharide composed of two monosaccharides – glucose and fructose – that are linked in chemical combination. These separate during digestion; the glucose molecules pass into the bloodstream through the small intestine and are distributed to the organs, where they are metabolized into energy (any surplus not needed for energy is stored in fat cells). Fructose, the sweetest natural sweetener, is mainly metabolized in the liver, where enzymes convert it into glucose.

Most plants contain sucrose, but the greatest concentrations are found in the *Saccharum* genus, a very tall bamboo-like member of the grass family. The genus likely originated in South or Southeast Asia and it consists of several species, each with numerous varieties. Only two species – *Saccharum robustum* and *S. spontaneum* – can propagate in the wild, and they contain comparatively little sugar. *S. robustum* originated on New Guinea, and from it indigenous peoples domesticated *S. officinarum* or Creole cane, which has a higher sugar content than other species. It was such a success that by about 8,000 years ago it had been widely disseminated to the Philippines, Indonesia, India, Southeast Asia and China. In India, *S. officinarum* hybridized with *S. spontaneum*, a cane native to South Asia, to create *S. barberi*, a common sugar cane cultivated in India. In China, *S. officinarum* hybridized again with *S. spontaneum*, this time creating *S. sinense*, a sugar cane commonly grown in southern China.

The 'eyes'
or 'nodes'
on sugar cane.

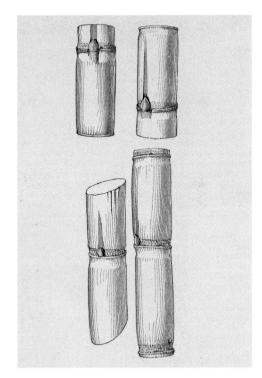

Humans have cultivated and tapped the sweet juice of various members of the *Saccharum* species for thousands of years, but *S. officinarum* has dominated the sugar cane industry, although other species and varieties have been used for breeding purposes since the late eighteenth century. Growing and processing cane is a labour-intensive activity. All domesticated canes are propagated asexually – sections of the stalk with at least one bud (also called an eye or node) are cut and planted. The cane fields had to be weeded and fertilized, and irrigated in many places. When ripe, the canes had to be cut down. These tasks were accomplished by hand until the invention of mechanical devices in the twentieth century.

Under ideal conditions, cane stalks can grow as much as 5 cm (2 inches) per day for several weeks. When mature, they are about 2 inches thick, and they grow to heights of 3.6 to 4.6 metres (12 to 15 feet). They reach their optimum sugar content at anywhere from nine to eighteen months. When the stem begins to flower, the sucrose is at its maximum level (ideally 17 per cent). The stalks are cut off just above the root in a process called 'ratooning'. The root then grows a new stalk, which will be lower in sugar content and less resistant to disease; still, stalks can be ratooned a few times before it is more efficient to remove the roots and plant new stem cuttings.

Humankind's dedication to the cultivation of sugar cane clearly demonstrates our millennia-old appreciation of its sweet taste. Initially people consumed the cane juice by simply chewing or sucking on pieces of stalk. It is difficult to preserve or store cut canes for any length of time: once cut, the stalk quickly deteriorates and turns into a brown mush. It is possible to squeeze the juice from the cane, but once exposed to air, it begins to ferment. This characteristic is a definite advantage if the desired end product is alcohol, but not helpful if what is wanted is a sweetener that can be preserved. How our ancestors worked out how to process cane juice so it could be preserved, and how the implementation and improvement of this process affected human history, is the subject of this book.

I

Early Sugar History

Extracting the sweet juice from sugar cane and turning it into crystals of sugar is a complicated process. There is little archaeological evidence to indicate just where or when cane juice was first converted into a form that could be preserved for longer periods of time. Most historians consider eastern India, about 2,500 years ago, the point of origin for the sugar industry. The main reason for this attribution is that many early Indian written sources mention cane sugar and its sweet juice. The *Mahābhāshya*, a commentary on Sanskrit grammar attributed to Patanjali and written some time between 400 and 200 BCE, includes recipes for rice pudding, barley meal and fermented beverages – all sweetened with some type of sugar.

Sugar is also mentioned in the *Arthaśātra*, Kautilya's classic Sanskrit work on Machiavellian statecraft dating to 324–300 BCE. This describes different sugar products, from *guda* (the least pure) to *khanda* (the source of the English word 'candy') to *śarkarā*, the purest sugar. The ancient *śarkarā* probably resembled the Indian sweetener, still used today, called jaggery – a coarse, solid sugar that retains some molasses as well as ash and other impurities. (The Sanskrit word *śarkarā* has, ironically, ended up in English as 'saccharin' – a sugar substitute.)

Early sugar products were made by crushing or grinding cane stalks using animal-powered mills fitted with stone wheels similar to those used to grind grain at the time. Crushing expelled the juice, which was then boiled to concentrate it. What's left is raw sugar, which is a sweet but dirty-brown semi-solid that does not ferment. Over time, innovators devised ways to filter out impurities, resulting in a whiter, sweeter and more crystalline product. The crystals could then be removed from the surrounding dark liquid and formed into soft balls. Later they were shaped into solid pieces of hard sugar and eventually these were ground into granulated sugar when needed. The coarse, dark liquid, later called molasses, was removed during the milling process. It could not be further refined into sugar using the technology of the time, but it, too, could be used as a sweetener and for making alcoholic beverages.

The advantages of refined sugar are immense. It can be granulated, pulverized, crystallized, melted, spun, pulled, boiled and moulded. It blends smoothly with other ingredients, either in a home kitchen or on an industrial production line. It can be used to mask the bitterness and enhance the properties of medicines. It is possible to preserve it for a long period of time, making a sweetener available throughout the year. Processed sugar had many culinary uses, such as concealing or enhancing flavours, making alcoholic beverages and preserving fruits and vegetables. Just as important, it could be transported to those regions where sugar cane could not grow, and thus became an important early commercial trade item.

Eastern India, where sugar cane was extensively grown and processed, was also the birthplace of Buddhism. According to Sucheta Mazumdar, author of *Sugar and Society in China* (1998), sugar cane was integrated into Buddhist religious rituals, and many sayings attributed to Buddha (563–483 BCE) include references to sugar cane. Sugary juices were not forbidden to monks observing a fast, and many Buddhist festival foods were made with sugar.

Sugar also appears frequently in other early religious sources, including Hindu works such as the *Buddhaghosa; or, Discourses on Moral Consciousness* (*c.* 500 CE), which describes sugar cane mills, the extracted juice, boiling the cane juice, raw sugar and lumps of sugar. Some sugar historians believe that these lumps were pliable, like toffee, rather than hard, while others consider this the first reference to crystalline sugar. Jain literature also mentions a sugar candy, which was particularly important for Jains, who do not consume honey because they believe that it consists of millions of living beings that would die if the honey were eaten.

Presuming that India was the point of origin for sugar manufacturing, it spread quickly to Southeast Asia and southern China. Little is known of the Southeast Asian operations with the exception that sugar – possibly in the form of sculptures – was exported to China by 221 BCE. There is more information available about the early sugar industry in China, where, legend has it, Buddhist monks introduced sugar cane and the process to make solid sugar. If the monks were not the first to introduce it, they clearly popularized it.

Sucrose, or cane syrup, was not China's first sweetener. In northern China, where grains were the dominant crops, a sweet syrup of maltose was made, mainly from sorghum. Maltose, a disaccharide composed of two glucose molecules, is much less sweet than sucrose. It was the most important sweetener in China and it is still used in Chinese cookery today.

The process for manufacturing sucrose was introduced into southern China by the third century BCE, but it was not commonly used in northern China until centuries later. The Chinese used sugar in medications as well as for sweetening food and beverages; they may have been the first to make rock candy. Cane sugar, however, was not considered a necessity and Chinese sugar processing did not evolve in the way it did in South Asia and, later, the Middle East. According to Marco Polo, who probably visited China at the end of the thirteenth century, the Mongol emperor of China, Kublai Khan, imported Egyptian sugar artisans to help teach the Chinese how to process sugar cane. Indeed, great progress on sugar growing, processing and preparing was made in the Middle East.

Sugar in the Middle East
and Mediterranean

The Greeks and Romans visited India in ancient times and became aware of Indian sugar. Nearchos, Alexander the Great's general who, in 327 BCE, sailed from the mouth of the Indus River to the mouth of the Euphrates in Asia Minor, reported in his *Indika* that 'a reed in India brings forth honey without the help of bees, from which an intoxicating drink is made though the plant bears no fruit.'

Small quantities of sugar made their way into the Mediterranean region during Roman times. These imports were used for medicinal purposes. Dioscorides, the first-century CE Greek physician and botanist, wrote in his five-volume *De Materia Medica*, 'There is a kind of concreted honey, called saccharon, found in reeds in India and Arabia Felix', which, he added, has the 'appearance of salt; and, like that, is brittle'. Galen, Seneca, Pliny and others reference a kind of honey imported from India, and many modern observers believe that this was in fact sugar. By the sixth century CE, sugar was shipped from India to a port on the Somali coast and then overland to

Alexandria, and from there, small quantities were traded to physicians, who used it for medical purposes.

Sugar cane was grown in Mesopotamia by 600 CE and commercial production began shortly thereafter. The Byzantine historian Theophanes recorded that blocks of *zuchar* were among the booty of great value captured in 622 in the campaigns by Heraklius against the Sassanid Empire. The Arabs had conquered Mesopotamia by 641, and through them sugar cane and its manufacturing process spread westward to the Nile River, the Nile Delta, the eastern Mediterranean and East Africa. It continued to be disseminated westward to the Mediterranean islands – Cyprus, Malta, Crete, Sicily and Rhodes – and sugar cane was widely grown in northern Africa, reaching southern Morocco by 682 CE. It was later grown in parts of southern Spain, southern Italy and Turkey.

In Mesopotamia the centre of the sugar industry was at the head of the Persian Gulf in the Tigris–Euphrates Delta. Sugar became a very important commodity in Baghdad, which at the time controlled an empire that extended from what is today Iran to Spain. Baghdad, with its estimated population of 1 million, was reportedly the largest city in the world. Ibn Sayyar Al-Warraq's tenth-century Baghdadi cookbook includes scores of recipes that have sugar as an ingredient. The sugar industry thrived until the arrival of the Mongols, who sacked Baghdad in 1258; the region fell into political disorder and sugar production was devastated, but by this time the sugar industry was well established in the Mediterranean.

Growing sugar cane and manufacturing sugar in the Middle East and the Mediterranean entailed heftier investments than in India. The hot, dry climates east of India required large irrigation systems to grow sugar cane. As these systems frequently extended over great distances, governments or very large landowners were needed to construct, maintain and regulate them. Also needed were customers who were willing and able to buy sugar – a very expensive luxury at the time.

Upper Egypt was particularly well positioned to grow sugar cane. With its good warm climate, plenty of water and rich soil in the Nile Delta, sugar became an important ingredient in Egyptian culinary life, at least among the wealthy. On occasion, however, sugar was also distributed to common people. Feasts often included sugar sculptures and guests, depending on their rank, were given between 1 and 25 lb (450 g – 11.3 kg) of sugar as gifts. Sugar was sold in markets throughout Upper Egypt, which became the major supplier of sugar to the Middle East and Europe. Sugar growers, millers and refiners grew wealthy.

As Europeans re-conquered the Mediterranean lands, such as Crete and Sicily, from the Muslims, they learned how to grow sugar cane and manufacture sugar. During the Crusades Europeans conquered Jerusalem, which they controlled from 1099 to 1187. Sugar production was a lucrative business in this area and Tyre (today in Lebanon) was an important sugar

Egyptian sugar mill in the Middle Ages.

Sicilian sugar mill, *c.* 14th century.

trading city. William of Tyre, who wrote a history of the kingdom of Jerusalem, proclaimed that sugar was a precious product 'very necessary for the use and health of mankind, which is carried by merchants to the most remote countries of the world'. Soldiers and pilgrims in the Near East were introduced to sugar, which they carried back to their home countries. This helped create a demand for sugar in Europe, where monarchs and other nobles, at least, enjoyed it.

Venice, an Italian city-state, had been importing and re-exporting sugar from the eastern Mediterranean since the tenth century. When the Crusades began in 1095, this trade became a very lucrative business. The Venetians expanded their control over Crete and extended their influence over other islands, such as Cyprus. Thanks in part to the sugar re-export business, the small city-state soon became one of the most important powers in the Mediterranean. Although Genoa would later become a central distribution point for Portuguese sugar from the Atlantic islands, it was Venice that dominated the sugar trade in the Mediterranean for almost 500 years.

A serious problem that restricted the growth of sugar production in Europe during the Middle Ages was the lack of labour. This was exacerbated by constant wars in sugar-producing areas of the Mediterranean, followed by the arrival of the Black Death (bubonic plague), which infected Europe from the 1340s. During the next several decades an estimated 30 to 60 per cent of the population of Europe died, creating a labour shortage. In addition, during this time there was an increasing migration from rural areas to cities, which added to the labour shortage in sugar-growing areas. Plantation owners in Sicily and other Mediterranean islands paid premium wages for farm workers, and jobs there were sought after by many Europeans. Still, there were not enough labourers, so plantation owners turned to slaves. Both Christian and Muslims used slaves to plant, harvest and process sugar. At first these were prisoners captured during military campaigns in what is today Bulgaria, Turkey and Greece, but slaves were also acquired from East and, later, West Africa.

Besides a diminished labour pool, Mediterranean sugar manufacturing had another serious limitation – climate. Sugar cane prefers tropical climates. A freeze, or even just a spell of cool weather, could limit the growth of the cane. A more serious problem was the lack of cheap, plentiful fuel to stoke the boilers that converted cane juice into refined sugar. The demand for firewood caused deforestation throughout the sugar-growing areas of the Mediterranean. Deforestation reduced soil fertility and water availability as rainwater flowed away, eroding unprotected soil. The sugar industry began to decline in the eastern Mediterranean – Lebanon, Syria, Egypt and Palestine – beginning in the fifteenth century; by the end of the century these areas were importing sugar. The sugar industry continued to thrive in Cyprus and Crete under Venetian control, and in the western Mediterranean for another century, before it too began to falter.

Yet another change in the eastern Mediterranean sugar trade was the rise of the Ottoman Turks. In 1453, they captured Constantinople, the capital of the Byzantine Empire; they then conquered the Middle East and North Africa and moved into Eastern Europe. The Turks controlled the overland trade routes between the east and the west, and when the trade was disrupted, European royalty and the upper classes were unable to easily import sugar, spices and other riches from Asia. Europeans began to explore ways of circumventing the Turks and Arabs.

Atlantic Sugar

Beginning in the fourteenth century, the Portuguese began exploring the eastern Atlantic, where they found and colonized islands such as Madeira and the nearby island of Porto Santo. Sugar plantations were established on these islands, and sugar was exported from them to Portugal by the mid-fifteenth century. Any excess not sold in Portugal was exported, generating a considerable profit, which encouraged more exploration and more sugar plantations.

Spain, too, explored the Atlantic and established a colony on the Canary Islands off the coast of northwest Africa. These islands had the advantage of a good climate for growing sugar cane and indigenous peoples who could be enslaved to run the mills. Sugar was exported from the Canaries to Spain by 1500. As was the case in the Mediterranean, lack of fuel was a problem; when the islands were deforested, the sugar industry faltered – and later collapsed due to stiff competition from cheap sugar producers elsewhere.

Optimal locations for growing sugar cane were the uninhabited islands of São Tomé and Príncipe in the Gulf of Guinea, off the coast of tropical Africa; the Portuguese had discovered them in 1470. They had an ideal climate, easy access to slaves in Africa, lots of water to irrigate the cane fields and plenty of fuel to run the mills. Sugar production ramped up, and even with the expenses of the long, arduous sail back to Portugal, it generated large profits for planters.

2

New World Sugar to 1900

Christopher Columbus was very familiar with the Atlantic islands and the sugar industry that thrived on them. As an agent for an Italian firm in Genoa, Columbus visited Madeira to purchase sugar in 1478. His first wife's father was the governor of Porto Santo. After Columbus's wife died, he married again, this time to a woman whose family owned a sugar estate on Madeira. When Columbus returned to Spain after his first voyage to the Caribbean, he was convinced that sugar cane would grow on the islands he had explored. On his second voyage to the Caribbean in 1493, Columbus stopped in the Canary Islands and picked up seed cane, which he introduced to the Caribbean island of Hispaniola (today Haiti and the Dominican Republic). Columbus and other Spanish explorers established settlements on other islands, such as Puerto Rico (1508), Jamaica (1509) and Cuba (1511). Sugar cane was planted on these islands, as it would be later in the Spanish and other European colonies of Central and South America.

Hispaniola was the most important New World sugar producer. Sugar was exported from the island to Spain by 1516; within 30 years, the island had 'powerful mills and four horse mills'. Spanish ships picked up 'cargoes of sugar and the skimmings and molasses that are lost would make a great

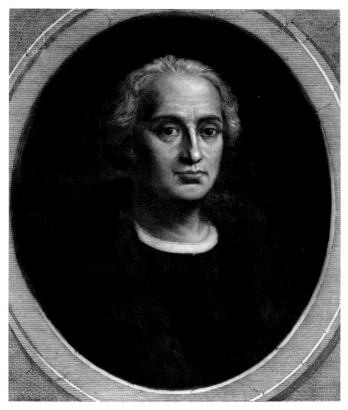

No image of the real Christopher Columbus has survived. This print was made in 1892 to celebrate the 400th anniversary of his discovery of America.

province rich', reported Gonzalo Fernández de Oviedo y Valdés, the contemporary chronicler of the island's history.

While the Caribbean had the perfect climate for growing cane and there was plenty of fuel and water, there was a shortage of manpower. Few Spaniards were willing to migrate to the New World to labour on sugar plantations. Indigenous peoples, such as the Taino and Carib tribes, had no interest in working on these plantations; when the Spanish enslaved them, they were understandably less than industrious. What with constant wars, and epidemics of communicable diseases brought over by the Europeans, an estimated 80 to 90 per cent of the indigenous population of the islands died off during the century following the first European encounter. The Caribbean sugar industry languished.

Brazil was a different story. The Portuguese had landed there in 1500 and later set up small coastal trading posts. It was also an ideal location for growing sugar: the climate was perfect and there was an abundance of fuel for the boilers, plenty of water and an unlimited amount of land. The indigenous people provided a potential supply of slave labour. Small sugar plantations called *engenhos* (the Portuguese word means 'mills', but was applied to the entire sugar plantation complex – fields, mills and factories) were established along the coast by 1520. By 1548, six *engenhos* were operating in Pernambuco; by 1583, there were 66, plus another 36 in nearby Bahia and still others in the southern region.

Portuguese sugar growers are credited with inventing or popularizing several crucial technological improvements. During the early seventeenth century, the *engenhos* adopted a new mill design that crushed cane between three vertically mounted rollers or cylinders. Cane would be fed into two rollers on one side, and then workers on the other side turned the cane back around through other rollers. This was a much more efficient process than the traditional mill press, which was promptly abandoned. The new style of mill could easily be powered by animals, water or even, in some cases, wind; it required fewer workers to operate it and much more sugar was produced as a result.

Yet another important technological change occurred in the process of refining sugar. Traditionally sugar mills had just one large cauldron, in which the cane juice was boiled until supersaturation occurred. The Brazilians created a multiple-cauldron system in which the liquid was ladled from one large cauldron into a series of three successively smaller vessels. This gave overseers much greater control over the process and permitted them to operate on a larger scale.

Brazilian sugar production rapidly escalated, but the industry encountered a major setback when its indigenous labour pool contracted. Disease and wars decimated the native population, and then the Catholic Church in Brazil began to oppose the enslavement of indigenous peoples. A solution soon appeared: the Portuguese sugar colony on São Tomé, which could not compete with the Brazilian sugar industry, shifted its business plan to exporting African slaves to Brazil. Initially many slaves were skilled workers who had worked in the sugar plantations on São Tomé. Later the slaves were any people who could be acquired in Africa and São Tomé served simply as a holding area and a point of departure for Portuguese ships that crisscrossed the Atlantic, transporting slaves to Brazil and elsewhere in the New World, and carrying sugar home to Europe. During the seventeenth century alone, an estimated 560,000 African slaves were shipped to Brazil and other European colonies in the Americas.

Brazilian sugar production intensified and large amounts were exported to Europe. By the late sixteenth century, sugar was Brazil's most important export, exceeding the production of the whole of the rest of the Atlantic world combined. Outpaced by Brazil's output, the Mediterranean sugar industry disappeared altogether and it rapidly declined on the Atlantic islands. Brazil dominated world sugar production.

Sugar Refining

Europeans separated the tasks of growing, processing and refining sugar. Growing and basic processing occurred in their colonies in the Atlantic and Americas, but the refining was accomplished in European cities. This division between producing and refining sugar had several advantages. First, it meant that colonial growing areas did not need local factories, which required large investments, to complete the refining process. Instead these refining centres could be centrally located in Europe's large cities, closer to their ultimate market. Second, transportation of sugar from tropical latitudes by ship was slow, and it was difficult to prevent spoilage en route to the home country. Shipping sugar in a less refined form reduced the risk of spoilage and also allowed European refiners to turn out exactly the kind of product their customers wanted. Finally, by completing the process in European cities, refiners generated some profit for the home country, rather than just for the colony. This final point reflects the economic philosophy of the day – mercantilism. It viewed colonies as places to supply raw materials to the home countries, where manufactured goods would be produced and sold back to its colonies.

Europe's premier refining city in the sixteenth century was Antwerp. Initially it controlled the trade in and refining of sugar from Portuguese and Spanish colonies. Thanks to sugar, Antwerp became Europe's richest and second largest city. It remained in this dominant position until 1576, when Spanish armies sacked it. Antwerp's sugar trade collapsed, as did the city's importance. Other European cities, such as London, Bristol, Bordeaux and Amsterdam, jumped into the void. They launched sugar-refining operations, and wealth flowed to them.

Caribbean Sugar

For almost a century, the Brazilian sugar industry dominated the Atlantic world's sugar trade, but it began to lose market share in the mid-seventeenth century when British, French and Dutch colonists established sugar plantations in the Americas. The Dutch established sugar plantations on the northern coast of South America in what would later become Surinam and the island of Curaçao. In 1630, the Dutch occupied Recife in Pernambuco and other Portuguese settlements in Brazil, which they retained for the next 24 years. The Dutch permitted Sephardic Jews to live and practise their religion openly in these settlements. The Dutch and the Jews became intimate with the growing and production of sugar cane. When the Portuguese retook the Dutch-occupied areas in Brazil, both the Jews and the Dutch left. Some settled in Barbados, a British colony.

Barbados was unoccupied when the British began to settle the island in 1627. Early colonists were mainly small farmers

Planting and hoeing sugar field in Antigua, 18th century.

Martinique sugar plantation during the 18th century.

who planned to make their fortunes by growing and curing tobacco. Unfortunately Virginia and other colonies produced more tobacco at less cost. It was the Dutch and Jewish refugees from Brazil who introduced sugar cane to Barbados and taught plantation owners how to convert the cane into sugar. Slaves were imported from Africa to grow the cane and operate the rapidly constructed mills. The island quickly focused on sugar production, as did St Kitts, the Leeward Islands and, later, Jamaica, after its conquest by the British in 1655.

Similarly the French started sugar colonies on the islands of Martinique and Guadeloupe in 1635, and established plantations on the western part of Hispaniola. In 1697, Spain and France signed the Treaty of Ryswyck, dividing the island of Hispaniola into French and Spanish territories. Over the next 100 years the French colony of Saint-Domingue (today Haiti) became the most productive sugar island in the Caribbean.

Large sugar-cane plantations emerged in the British West Indies. Growers paid their expenses by selling molasses and rum to England or to the English colonies in North America. The sale of these by-products made the islands' prodigious

Slaves cutting sugar cane, from *Ten Views in the Island of Antigua* (1823).

sugar production almost pure profit. Some growers made such huge fortunes in sugar that they installed overseers to run their plantations and then sailed home to England, where they purchased large estates. Sugar also brought wealth to many merchants, refiners, shippers, bankers, insurers, investors and distillers in Britain. By 1760, the city of Bristol alone had twenty sugar refineries that annually processed 831,600 lb (377,200 kg) of sugar cane. Sugar barons and their allies in England emerged as a powerful political force that influenced Parliament throughout the eighteenth and early nineteenth centuries. Their financial self-interest diverged from that of their counterparts in the British colonies in North America. The economic and political conflict began with molasses.

Molasses and Rum

To sustain the rapidly expanding slave populations in the West Indies, food and other essentials had to be imported, mostly from British colonies in North America. In return molasses, raw sugar and rum were shipped from the West Indies. Molasses, a by-product of the sugar refining process, was a much cheaper sweetener than crystallized white sugar. It could also be used to make alcoholic beverages, and plantation owners and merchants used it in the production of high-quality rum, which they exported to England or sent to Africa in exchange for slaves.

Rum was also made on the French islands in the Caribbean, but French brandy producers objected to the importation of rum into metropolitan France. The French West Indies sugar industry ended up with a massive excess of molasses. Rather than dump it into the sea, the French government permitted its colonies to sell molasses to anyone who would buy it. The obvious market was the British colonies in North America.

Since molasses from the French West Indies cost 60 to 70 per cent less than the product from the British West Indies, New England colonial ships acquired it in bulk from Martinique, Guadeloupe and Saint-Domingue. New England was ideally suited for rum production: it had skilled workers needed to make the stills, an abundance of ships to transport the bulky molasses and plenty of wood for fuelling stills and making barrels. Rum quickly became the distilled beverage of choice in North America. By 1700, New England was importing more molasses from French colonies than from British ones. In exchange for the molasses and raw sugar, American merchants sent lumber, fish (mainly salt cod for slaves) and other provisions.

As a result of this trade, British West Indian sugar growers lost business, so much so that from 1716 they began to urge the British Parliament to restrict New England's imports of sugar and molasses from French and other European colonies in the Caribbean. Their proposed laws would give the British West Indies a complete monopoly on the molasses and sugar trade, allowing sugar-cane growers to set their own prices and make substantially greater profits. Parliament finally passed the Molasses Act in 1733. The law placed a duty of sixpence per pound on sugar, molasses, rum and spirits imported from non-British colonies.

Had the Molasses Act been enforced, it would likely have crippled New England's fishing and lumber businesses, because these products were traded to Spanish, French and Dutch West Indian possessions. Enforcement would also have hindered the slave trade, in which some New Englanders were involved. But passing the Molasses Act and enforcing it were two different things. The only enforcement provision in the law required the tax to be collected by local customs officials, who were often friends of those engaged in the molasses trade. Customs officials were also few in number and could easily be bribed to look the other way as smugglers shipped in molasses through the thousands of coves along the New England coastline where goods could be landed undetected.

In the 1730s, Parliament permitted growers in the British West Indies to trade sugar directly with countries in Europe. The growers' fortunes improved and they stopped pressing for enforcement of the Molasses Act. Even so, the act remained on the statute books for the next 30 years, during which time molasses was openly smuggled into North America. It was a major misstep to pass the Molasses Act and not enforce it – a blunder that would have serious repercussions later.

American Sugar

In 1725, New York launched its first sugar refinery, and sugar producers in the Caribbean began to ship raw sugar to the city. This partially refined cane sugar was sweeter and more expensive than molasses, but unlike molasses it could be refined into pure sugar. Other refineries were soon established in New York, where they were the largest buildings in the city, and sugar refining became one of the city's most lucrative industries.

As a result of the Seven Years War (1756–63), England acquired vast new possessions in North America – and the ongoing expense of defending them. To generate revenue, Parliament passed the Sugar Act, which lowered the levy on imported molasses to its American colonies that had been imposed 30 years before. As this was a decrease on the existing duty, no one in the British Parliament thought there would be any concern in its American colonies. But the act also included strong enforcement provisions, such as stationing British warships to patrol the coast and sending British custom officials to American ports to enforce the collection of duties.

By the time the Sugar Act was passed, New Englanders had been smuggling molasses and other contraband for 30 years. Enforcement of the Sugar Act made smuggling much more risky. Americans protested the Sugar Act and, in support, many merchants in Boston and New York agreed to stop buying British imports. The Act was repealed, but the colonial resistance set Parliament on a course for more laws to enforce its taxing authority in British North America, and these in turn created even bigger colonial protests. The result was a military conflict, which broke out in 1775.

The American sugar trade and refining businesses collapsed during the war, since the British Navy sporadically controlled the oceans. New York City, the centre of American sugar refining, was occupied by British forces for eight years, and sugar production collapsed. When the war ended, the sugar trade resumed. New York's sugar-refining industry quickly revived and then expanded as raw sugar flooded in from the Caribbean. In 1803, the United States purchased from France the vast tract known as Louisiana. Sugar cane had been grown in the southernmost tip of the Territory – around the Mississippi Delta – since the 1750s, but it was at the northern fringe of the crop's growing range; rainfall was irregular and the growing season was relatively short for sugar cane – only ten months. The cane had to be harvested in the autumn lest freezing temperatures destroy the crop. In 1795, Jean-Etienne Boré, a Frenchman, imported Haitian slaves who were knowledgeable about growing and processing sugar cane. With their help, Boré's plantation did well, and other sugar refineries were constructed. By 1812, the territory had 75 sugar mills in operation. The industry received a major boost in 1817, when ribbon cane was introduced; this plant matured faster than the variety that had previously been planted. The 1820s saw a tremendous growth in sugar-cane cultivation, exploiting the ample supply of slave labour and supported by federal tariffs on imported sugar. Thanks to cheap sugar, America's annual consumption per capita rose from 13 lb (5.9 kg) in 1831 to 30 lb (13.6 kg) by mid-century.

Throughout the nineteenth century, most American sugar was refined in New York, which was an ideal location for the industry. Its port facilities were the best on the East Coast, facilitating the shipping of raw sugar from the Caribbean and Louisiana. New York itself had a large market for sugar, and the city's road, canal and later train connections meant that refined products could easily be shipped north, south and west. The German-born William Havemeyer, who had been an apprentice at a London sugar refinery, immigrated to America and in 1799 began running the Edmund Seaman & Co. sugar refinery in New York City; six years later, he opened his own refinery with his brother. It was only one of several refineries operating in the city at the time – and more were soon to be launched. In 1864, the Havemeyer family built the largest and most technologically advanced sugar refinery in the world in Williamsburg on Long Island.

As manufacturing methods improved and production rose dramatically, sugar prices dropped steeply. In 1887, the Havemeyers and seven other sugar industry leaders formed the Sugar Trust; their intention was to curtail production in order to raise prices and profits for all the companies. Following the acquisition of more companies, the resulting conglomerate was named the American Sugar Refining Company. Inefficient plants were closed while others were combined, and American Sugar Refining unofficially but effectively fixed the price of refined sugar. In 1900, the company created a subsidiary, Domino

Domino sugar was the largest-selling sugar brand in America during the 20th century.

Sugar, to market the parent company's refined sugar. By 1907, the American Sugar Refining Company controlled 97 per cent of all production of refined sugar in America.

Sugar and Slavery

Until the mid-nineteenth century, the entire sugar industry in the Americas was based on slavery. Slaves were acquired from Africa and transported to the Americas to be exchanged for sugar, which was exported to England, where the ships then took on goods to be exchanged for slaves in Africa. The slaves were then transported to the Caribbean to work on sugar plantations. This became known as the 'Triangle Trade'.

Slaves on sugar plantations were subjected to long hours of strenuous work in cane fields, mills and factories. Their lives were cut short by heavy workloads, poor diet, rampant diseases such as yellow fever and the lack of medical care. Some slaves, particularly in Brazil and Jamaica, escaped and formed their own communities in the interior. Workers who died or disappeared had to be replaced, and in the first 75 years of the eighteenth century, the West Indies alone absorbed 1.2 million African slaves. An estimated 252,000 slaves arrived in Barbados and another 662,400 in Jamaica during the period from 1700 to 1810. Slaves soon outnumbered Europeans, particularly on the Caribbean islands. In the French colony of Saint-Dominique, in 1789, a white minority numbering only 32,000 controlled an estimated 500,000 slaves.

Slave revolts, a regular occurrence in Brazil and the Caribbean, were put down violently, with the rebels usually put to death in a gruesome manner. The only successful slave revolt, in Saint-Dominique, began in 1791. Inspired by the ideals of the French Revolution and the Declaration of the Rights

The remains of a sugar factory in Haiti, *c.* 1830, which was destroyed during slave uprisings in the early 19th century.

of Man, which proclaimed that all men were free and equal, slaves on Saint-Dominique rebelled against their masters. France sent armies to the island to quell the revolt, but the soldiers were defeated by yellow fever and the guerrilla tactics of their opponents. The rebels finally prevailed in 1803, and on 1 January 1804, Haiti became an independent republic, the second in the Americas. Throughout the rebellion, white plantation owners and overseers who were not killed outright fled the colony, some to Louisiana, others to Cuba. Haiti's sugar industry, previously the most productive in the Caribbean, never recovered.

Opposition to slavery grew in Europe and North America in the late eighteenth century. Quakers and others abstained from consuming sugar made with slave labour, but abstention remained an isolated and individual tactic. When Parliament failed to pass the slave trade abolition bill in 1791, British abolitionists joined together to boycott slave-grown sugar. Since one obvious place where sugar was consumed was the tea table, women took an active role in the abstention movement. It developed a broad base of support, attracting as many as 400,000 supporters. Slavery opponents were not just abolitionists: there were also liberal economists, such as Adam Smith, author of *The Wealth of Nations* (1776), who argued that the costs of slavery far outweighed any financial gain. Others were concerned with the undue political power of West Indian planters, who had skewed Parliamentary bills in their favour to the detriment of the British economy throughout the eighteenth century.

The growth of the abolition movement in England encouraged the importation and consumption of slave-free sugar from India. At the time, little Indian sugar was transported to England, but as the abolition movement picked up steam more orders were placed and by the early nineteenth century sugar from India was generally available in

Isaac Cruikshank, 'The Gradual Abolition off the Slave Trade, – or Leaving of Sugar by Degrees', 1792.

Abolitionist broadside promoting Indian sugar not made by slaves.

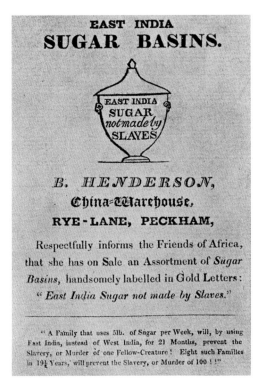

EAST INDIA

SUGAR BASINS.

EAST INDIA
SUGAR
not made by
SLAVES

B. HENDERSON,
China-Warehouse,
RYE - LANE, PECKHAM,

Respectfully informs the Friends of Africa, that she has on Sale an Assortment of *Sugar Basins*, handsomely labelled in Gold Letters: *" East India Sugar not made by Slaves."*

" A Family that uses 5lb. of Sugar per Week, will, by using East India, instead of West India, for 21 Months, prevent the Slavery, or Murder of one Fellow-Creature! Eight such Families in 19½ Years, will prevent the Slavery, or Murder of 100 ! !"

England. Quakers established 'Free Produce Societies', which sold Asian sugar.

In the United States, abolitionists tried to grow sugar beet and abstain from purchasing sugar imported from the Caribbean. American Quakers also supported the maple sugar industry as an alternative, and small amounts of maple sugar were produced beginning in the 1780s. In 1789, Philadelphians agreed to buy a given amount of maple sugar at fixed prices to help the industry get off the ground. Quakers especially urged the use of maple sugar to 'reduce by that much the lashings the Negroes have to endure to grow cane sugar to satisfy our gluttony'. Almanacs urged readers to make maple sugar at home because it was sweeter than cane sugar, which was 'mingled with the groans and tears of slavery'. In the 1830s, articles in the *Episcopal Recorder* and the *Colored American* newspaper urged parents to prevent their children from purchasing sweets in confectionery shops because all purchases of sugar supported 'the whole iniquity' of slavery.

Abstention and other abolition efforts finally brought some success. On 3 March 1807, President Thomas Jefferson signed a bill 'to prohibit the importation of slaves into any port or place within the jurisdiction of the United States'. Three weeks later, the British House of Lords passed an Act for the Abolition of the Slave Trade. Slavery continued in the British West Indies until 1834, in the French colonies until 1848, and in the United States until 1866. Cubans held slaves until 1886 and Brazilians did so until 1888.

Technological improvements – such as the vacuum pan, the centrifuge and the application of steam power to the sugar refineries in the late nineteenth century – made production less labour intensive, but large numbers of labourers were still needed. Freed slaves were unwilling to work in sugar plantations after emancipation. The demand for a workforce led the sugar industry to engage in hiring contract labourers, particularly from India and China, to work the plantations. Eventually hundreds of thousands of contract workers flooded into sugar-growing areas, and many remained after their contracts were completed.

Cuban Sugar

The immediate beneficiary of the end of the sugar industry in Saint-Domingue was Cuba, a Spanish colony. Sugar cane had been grown on the island since 1523, but the industry did not mature because of Spain's policies, which included laws that forbade Cubans from trading with foreign ships and restrictions on importing slaves.

The Cuban sugar industry did not get off the ground until 1762, when the English controlled Havana for ten months during the Seven Years War. During this period the British introduced tens of thousands of slaves into Cuba. When the war ended, the British withdrew, but Cuban sugar producers demanded liberalized policies: Spain relaxed its laws regarding the importation of slaves and permitted Cubans to trade with foreign countries. More than 18,000 slaves were brought to Cuba during the 1780s, and more than 125,000 during the 1790s and the first decade of the nineteenth century. The Cuban sugar industry thrived, considerable amounts were exported and finished goods from Europe and the United States flowed into Cuba. Still, in 1790, Cuba produced only 15,000 tons of sugar. But this was about to change.

During the slave revolt in Saint-Domingue, Frenchmen from that island moved to Cuba with their slaves and set up sugar plantations and factories. Sugar production in Cuba was enhanced by an improved transportation system; new roads and, later, railways made it possible to move sugar from the refineries to seaports for export. Simultaneously sugar production on other Caribbean islands decreased, largely because of the emancipation of slaves in the British- and French-controlled islands. Cuba retained slavery and quickly became the most cost-efficient sugar producer in the world. Sugar became Cuba's premier export crop, and the United States became its major trading partner. Small sugar mills were closed, and more efficient central factories began to service several cane growers. Cuban sugar received another boost during the American Civil War (1861–5), when sugar plantations in Louisiana were crippled and there was a jump in sugar's price on the world market. From the 1840s to the 1870s, Cuba supplied 25 to 40 per cent of the world's total sugar.

The Cuban sugar industry stagnated during a rebellion on the island that lasted from 1868 to 1878. During the war, many sugar producers left Cuba and some set up shop in the Dominican Republic. After Cuban slaves were emancipated in 1886, many slaves left plantations and refused to work in the sugar industry. Cuba reached out to contract labourers. During the following decades, it absorbed 1.2 million immigrants from Spain, the United States, China, Haiti and other Caribbean islands.

Yet another serious problem was increased competition from abroad in the form of sugar beet, which was grown and converted into refined sugar in Europe and the United States. But large American corporations increasingly invested in Cuban sugar refining. In 1890, they lobbied the United States Congress to pass the McKinley Tariff Act, which eliminated tariffs on refined sugar imported from Cuba. By 1896, the Sugar Trust alone owned nineteen Cuban sugar refineries.

Cutting sugar cane in Cuba, from *Commercial Cuba: A Book for Businessmen . . . Illustrated* (1899).

Cuban sugar factory, 19th century.

Exports of Cuban sugar to the United States soared, as did American exports of finished goods to Cuba. Production hit 1.1 million tons in 1894. But then sugar-beet growers and American sugar refiners successfully lobbied Congress to levy a 40 per cent increase in duties on imported Cuban sugar. Spain retaliated by placing a tariff on American goods exported to Cuba. The price of Cuban raw sugar dropped sharply, while prices for imported goods from the United States soared. Workers on sugar plantations were laid off, and many joined Cuban guerrilla groups who were fighting for independence from Spain. Guerrillas destroyed sugar refineries as well as cane fields, and the Spanish colonial authorities retaliated with harsh measures, including creating concentration camps, to put down the revolt. The resulting atrocities were covered by many American newspapers; inflammatory articles, which came to be known as 'yellow journalism', swayed u.s. public opinion in favour of the guerrillas.

The Spanish American War and Its Aftermath

In February 1898, an American battleship, the USS *Maine*, exploded and sank in Havana harbour. Although the cause was never determined, the Americans blamed the Spanish. Two months after the explosion, the United States declared war on Spain. In five months of conflict, the American military occupied Cuba, Puerto Rico, Guam and the Philippines. The United States also annexed Hawaii, then controlled by American sugar interests.

After the war, sugar output in Puerto Rico, Hawaii and the Philippines increased to some extent, but Cuban production skyrocketed with the advent of new milling methods, such as the use of water mills, enclosed furnaces, steam engines and improved vacuum pans. American investments in Cuban sugar also soared. By 1919, Americans were estimated to control about 40 per cent of the Cuban sugar industry. Cuban sugar production hit 3.5 million tons by 1925.

Cutting cane, early 20th century.

Looking Backwards

During the four centuries after Columbus's first voyage to the Caribbean in 1492, the sugar industry had greatly changed. It had shifted from the Mediterranean and the Atlantic islands to the Americas. Plantation labour had shifted from a slave-based force to one based on contract workers. Sugar harvesting, milling and processing had emerged from a largely hand-powered system to an industrial one based on machinery and the latest technology that science could devise. Sugar production had shifted from small plantations and mills to one based on multinational corporations. All of these developments contributed to the steep decline in the price of sugar and the rapid rise in its consumption throughout the world.

3
Global Sugar

The beet (*Beta vulgaris*) originated around the Mediterranean, and both the roots and the leaves were widely consumed in Europe and the Middle East beginning in Neolithic times. The Greeks and Romans grew it in their gardens. Medical practitioners prescribed it as the remedy for various ailments. Beets survived as a garden plant during the Middle Ages and they were grown all over Europe by the fifteenth century. Sixteenth-century herbals list several varieties of beet, including pale ones with a sweet taste. The French agronomist Olivier de Serres, in his *Théâtre d'agriculture* (1600), was the first observer to report that the root of the beet 'is counted among the choice foods and the juice which it yields on cooking is like a sugar syrup'.

Beets are a sturdy food crop. Unlike sugar cane, they grow in temperate climates; the hardy plants can withstand droughts and floods. Their growing season is relatively short, so another crop can be planted after they have been harvested. The roots (beetroot) can be dried and preserved for later consumption, and they make excellent fodder for cattle and horses. They became a common agricultural crop in Europe during the seventeenth century.

It was a Prussian chemist named Andreas S. Marggraf who discovered another important property of beetroots. In

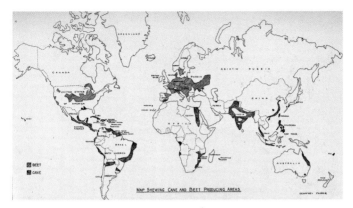

Sugar cane- and beet-growing areas around the world in the 1930s.

1747, Marggraf presented a paper to the Academy of Sciences in Berlin reporting that he had derived small amounts of sucrose from them. The variety of beet that Marggraf used in his experiment, however, yielded very little sugar, and the extraction process was neither practical nor economical. Still, it was promising: if this process could be improved, non-tropical countries would be able to supply their own sugar and would not have to import it. The Prussian government funded research into beet sugar production sporadically for the next several decades.

Marggraf repeated his experiments in 1761 and made enough sugar to produce a few loaves, but the process remained impractical from a commercial standpoint. After Marggraf's death, in 1782, his student Franz Carl Achard continued experimenting with beets and found that some varieties yielded more sugar than others. He perfected Marggraf's process and in 1799 gave Frederick William III, the king of Prussia, a few pounds of sugar crystallized from beetroot. Two years later, the king gave Achard financial assistance to construct a factory in Silesia to test his method. Achard learned a great deal about

Franz Carl Achard (1753–1821).

beets and he is credited with being the first person to extract sugar from them on a commercial basis. He determined that white beetroots contained the most sucrose, and they were subsequently used for breeding purposes. Achard claimed that domestically produced beet sugar could be more economical than imported cane sugar, but he was unable to make a success of his factory.

The beet sugar industry revived during the Napoleonic Wars, when France enforced the Continental System, which prevented goods from Great Britain or its colonies from entering European countries that were controlled by or allied with France. This included imported sugar from the

British West Indies, which had previously flooded Europe. In 1791, the slave revolt in the French colony of Saint-Dominique greatly reduced the amount of sugar imported from French colonies in the Caribbean. During wartime, the British blockaded continental ports controlled by France, making it difficult for sugar to be imported from any source. France offered a bounty for the production of sugar from beets, and more than 100 sugar-beet factories were established, mainly in northern France, but also elsewhere in continental Europe. Sugar was successfully extracted, but the industry collapsed when peace was restored in 1815 and cheap sugar once again flowed in from the Caribbean.

But sugar beet was not forgotten. Vilmorin, a French seed producer and a pioneer in the selective breeding of plants, began breeding experiments aimed at increasing the sugar content of beets. In 1837, the company introduced the sugar beet (*B. vulgaris* var. *altissima*), which had a high sucrose content. Simultaneously new extraction techniques were developed

Achard's sugar beet factory in Silesia.

that lowered the cost of producing sugar from beets. The beet sugar industry revived in Germany, France, Belgium, Austro-Hungary, Russia and Scandinavia. Eventually breeders were able to produce beets with roots that were 20 per cent sucrose.

Even with this increase in sugar content and improved methods of extraction, it was still cheaper to import cane sugar than it was to extract beet sugar. Early support for beet sugar production came from Quakers and abolitionists, who opposed buying cane sugar produced with slave labour. This support died down in England and France when slaves in the Caribbean were emancipated in the mid-nineteenth century. Sugar prices should have escalated with the end of slavery in the Caribbean, but expanding sugar beet and cane production worldwide meant that prices declined throughout the nine-teenth century. National governments interested in supporting their sugar-beet industries created policies that favoured in-country beet growers by placing high tariffs and quotas on

Napoleon was ridiculed for his support of the sugar beet industry.

Field of ripe sugar beet, 1930s.

Children working in a sugar beet field in Sugar City, Colorado, in 1915.

Maple syrup remains an important sweetener in Canada and the United States, as in this illustration from *Upper Canada Sketches* by Thomas Conant (1898).

imported sugar. With governmental intervention, beet sugar cultivation in Europe expanded and hundreds of factories were opened during the late nineteenth century. Governmental support continued through the twentieth century, and Europe became a net exporter of sugar by the end of that century.

Sugar beet was also grown in the Americas, and attempts to convert it into sugar began as early as the 1830s. Successful operations, however, did not get off the ground until the 1870s in the United States and the 1880s in Canada. With governmental protection and support, sugar-beet operations rapidly expanded during the early twentieth century. Technological advancements, such as mechanical harvesting, increased production and efficiency.

African, Asian and Oceanian Sugar

As sugar-beet cultivation grew in temperate areas of the world, sugar-cane growing and manufacturing expanded in tropical Africa, Asia and the Pacific. Mauritius, a British colony in the Indian Ocean that had been acquired during the Napoleonic Wars, had the perfect tropical climate for growing sugar cane, which was introduced in 1829. As the industry grew, however, it faced serious labour shortages. The British plantation owners' solution was to contract with workers, and tens of thousands came from India. By the mid-nineteenth century, the island was producing 9.4 per cent of the world's sugar, and as sugar production declined in the West Indies, Mauritius became one of Britain's major suppliers. Rather than returning to India after their contract was up, most workers remained on Mauritius. When it became independent in 1975, the majority of its population was of Indian descent. Mauritius continues to grow sugar cane, with the European Union its major buyer.

Sugar cane was also grown in Natal, which today is part of South Africa. The cane growing area expanded into adjacent Zululand (today KwaZulu-Natal) after its annexation in 1887. Once again, the growers' main problem was finding a suitable workforce: Africans were not willing to work under the conditions and wages the growers offered. Workers were bought in India, but they, too, found the work disagreeable and shifted to other employment. Many remained in South Africa and opened other businesses instead of returning to India. Indians were replaced by African migrants from other parts of southern Africa, including large numbers of children, from Natal, KwaZulu and Mozambique.

Sugar cane was introduced into the Pacific islands in prehistoric times by Polynesians and Melanesians, who brought it with them as they set out on long voyages. When they reached new islands, they planted the cane. The British first planted sugar cane in Australia in 1788. It was originally brought to Sydney, but the climate there was too cold to grow it. In the 1860s, sugar production was relaunched. In Queensland, convict labour was used at first; New South Wales hired contract workers from Polynesia. In Queensland, sugar-cane growing was launched by small farmers, but this shifted to plantation-style cane growing in the 1880s, using contract labour from Melanesia. Queensland converted large sections of forested land to agricultural uses, with sugar as a leading crop.

By 1900, the sugar industry was one of America's most important businesses: cane was widely grown in Louisiana and Texas and in the newly acquired territories of Puerto Rico, the Philippines and Hawaii; sugar beet was grown in western states such as Utah and California. Sugar refining played an even greater role in many eastern cities. The most important was the Havemeyer operations in New York. As discussed previously, in 1887, Henry O. Havemeyer devised a partnership with other sugar refiners to be called the Sugar Refineries Company, commonly known as the Sugar Trust.

The American firm Ladd & Co. leased land on Kauai to grow and mill sugar in 1835; others followed its example. Few native Hawaiians wanted to work on sugar plantations, so the growers looked abroad for cheap labour and began to import contract workers, initially Chinese men (women were intentionally excluded). By 1860, Hawaii had 29 sugar plantations, and most of the territory's sugar exports went to the United States. When Mark Twain visited the islands in 1866, he was so impressed with the cane growing that he declared Hawaii 'the king of the sugar world far as astonishing productiveness is concerned'. In 1875, Hawaii and the United States signed a Reciprocity Treaty permitting duty-free importation of Hawaiian sugar.

California and Hawaii Sugar Company factory, early 1900s.

The following year, Claus Spreckels, a German immigrant who operated a beet sugar factory in California, arrived in Hawaii and immediately made arrangements to purchase most of the Hawaiian sugar. He eventually owned or controlled most of the sugar production in California and on the islands until the 1880s.

By 1882, Chinese labourers totalled 49 per cent of the entire sugar industry's workforce in Hawaii, and Hawaii's political leaders became concerned about the large number of foreigners living there. The following year, Hawaii stopped accepting immigrants from China, and most Chinese workers left. In 1887, American sugar interests forced the king of Hawaii to agree to a constitution giving them most of the power in the kingdom. With the assistance of u.s. Marines, Euro-American business interests overthrew the monarchy in 1893. They then put pressure on the United States Congress to annex the islands, which it finally did in 1898, during the Spanish–American War.

Labour was needed to work the cane fields and operate the refineries. Okinawan, Korean, Puerto Rican, Portuguese and Filipino nationals came to Hawaii to work in the sugar industry, but the largest group was Japanese immigrants, who had been coming to Hawaii as contract workers since 1865. When their contracts expired, many Japanese labourers remained in Hawaii, and their progeny are the largest single ethnic group on the islands today.

The California and Hawaii Sugar Company (C&H Sugar), formed in 1906, dominated sugar production in Hawaii until the 1930s, when sugar plantations were converted to other uses. Today, only one cane grower remains on the islands. C&H Sugar is now part of American Sugar Refining (Domino Sugar), a company owned by Florida Crystals and the Sugar Cane Growers Cooperative of Florida.

Florida is not an ideal place to grow sugar. Its semitropical climate has occasional freezes, which can destroy the cane crop.

Filling sugar bags in a California and Hawaii Sugar Company factory.

The southern part of the state would be preferable, but much of it is occupied by the Everglades National Park. Sugar plantations and mills had been established in eastern Florida in the late nineteenth century. Spain ceded Florida to the United States in 1821, and the sugar-cane industry rapidly expanded, but the plantations stagnated as they could not compete with domestic sugar from Louisiana or cheap imports from the Caribbean.

Sugar cane didn't get a second foothold in Florida until the 1930s, when the u.s. Sugar Corporation was launched in Clewiston. It remained a marginally successful company until 1942, when the Second World War drove up the demand for sugar and sugar cane was planted on even more acres, and this was just the beginning. In 1948, the Army Corp of Engineers began to drain the Everglades and establish an irrigation system to protect populated areas of southern Florida from storm damage. During the next 50 years, more than half of the Everglades was drained, and the reclaimed land became the Everglades Agricultural Area. While anything could have been planted there, the local climate – and federal subsidies – encouraged farmers to grow sugar cane.

When Fidel Castro took control of Cuba in 1959, the u.s. drastically reduced purchases of Cuban sugar. In retaliation, Castro nationalized Cuba's sugar operations, many of which were owned by Americans. The u.s. responded by halting all imports of Cuban sugar in 1961. Many wealthy Cuban sugar growers and processors, such as the Fanjul family, fled Cuba and bought land in southern Florida, where they planted sugar cane. The Fanjuls also acquired sugar plantations in the Dominican Republic.

In 1962, the u.s. Sugar Corporation opened the Bryant Sugar House near West Palm Beach, Florida. It was the world's most modern mill. By the early 1980s, u.s. Sugar was the largest sugar producer in the state and Florida was the number one sugar-producing state in America. Part of the reason for this success was the u.s. Department of Agriculture, which since 1979 has given subsidies and 'non-recourse' loans (which do not have to be repaid) to domestic growers, and imposed import quotas on sugar from the Dominican Republic, Brazil and the Philippines.

Subsidies went disproportionately to the largest cane growers and sugar-beet farmers. In 1991, 42 per cent of the subsidies went to 1 per cent of the growers. As a result of limited competition from abroad and domestic subsidies, American consumers have paid from eight to fourteen cents per pound above the world market price for sugar since 1985 – and that's on top of the subsidies they paid for through their taxes. Since sugar is added to many processed foods, these subsidies contribute to a hefty increase in the cost of food. The subsidies, quotas and tariffs did encourage sugar production in the United States: by 2000, 60 per cent of the raw sugar consumed in America was produced from domestic sources.

Since 2008, thanks to the North American Free Trade Association, Mexico can more easily export sugar into the United States and Canada without paying duties. This has sparked an increase in Mexican sugar-cane growing and refining. Today, Mexico is the seventh largest sugar producer in the world and in 2013–14 it supplied about 15 per cent of the sugar that Americans consumed.

War and Revolution

During the Spanish–American War in 1898, the u.s. Army occupied Cuba. In 1903, Cuba gained its independence, and the two countries signed the Reciprocity Agreement, which, among other provisions, provided for a 20 per cent reduction in the tariff on Cuban sugar imported into the United States. Even with the tariff, Cuban sugar continued to outsell sugar produced in America. During the following decade, Cuba became the dominant foreign supplier of sugar to the United States. American companies, such as the Czarnikow Rionda Company and the Cuban Trading Company, acquired Cuban sugar operations. In 1936, Alfonso Fanjul Sr, the heir to these companies, married into a major Cuban sugar family, and the combined resources became the biggest sugar operation in Cuba and one of the largest in the world.

As the American sugar beet industry expanded, sugar prices fell. The Depression hit in 1929, and Congress passed

Cutting cane on a Cuban sugar plantation, 1904.

Puck magazine cover with Cuba turning away from Uncle Sam, who is offering her a plate labelled 'Reduction of Tariff on Cuban Sugar', 1902.

the Smoot-Hawley Tariff Act to protect the domestic sugar industry by raising tariffs on imported sugar. The Cuban sugar industry suffered as prices plummeted. In 1934, the U.S. Congress took control of sugar imports and supported domestic production and refining by passing the Sugar Act (Jones-Costigan Act). After the Second World War, however, Cuban sugar imports picked up again, representing between 25 per cent and 51 per cent of all sugar consumed in the United States.

Cuba nationalized its sugar industry in 1961, and the confiscated plantations became state-run operations. Workers were promised permanent employment, and the government pressured them to achieve production targets, but with no financial incentive, productivity declined. In 1968, the crop was such a disaster that Cuba militarized the harvest to make sure production goals were met.

When the United States stopped importing sugar from Cuba in 1960, the Soviet Union and Eastern European countries picked up the slack: during the next 30 years they bought an estimated 87 per cent of Cuban sugar. When the Soviet Union collapsed in 1991, so did much of the Cuban sugar industry: of the country's 156 sugar mills, 71 closed and 60 per cent of cane fields were converted into vegetable farms or cattle ranches. However, with the invention of a process to make ethanol (a type of alcohol that can fuel vehicles) from sugar cane, the Cuban sugar industry has been revitalized in the twenty-first century.

British Sugar

Until the mid-seventeenth century, Britain was content to import raw sugar from the Mediterranean and the Atlantic

English boiling house, *c.* 1700s.

Illustration of the process from cutting the cane to its refining in London, c. 1830s.

islands, bringing it to London and other cities for refining. In the mid-1600s, Britain moved from buying sugar from other European nations to acquiring colonies in the West Indies, including Barbados and Jamaica, which became major sugar producers. In the nineteenth century, British businessmen established sugar-growing and refining operations in other diverse places such as Mauritius in the Indian Ocean, Natal in southern Africa, and Queensland in northeastern Australia.

During the mid-nineteenth century, sugar refining in Britain was dominated by two businessmen: Henry Tate and Abraham Lyle. Tate, a successful grocer in Liverpool, became a partner in the John Wright & Co. sugar refinery in that city. Tate took over the company in 1869 and renamed it Henry Tate & Sons. He opened additional refineries in Liverpool and in Silvertown, London, where sugar cubes were manufactured.

Tate's main competitor was the Scottish businessman Abram Lyle, who with partners acquired the Glebe Sugar Refinery in Greenock, Scotland, in 1865, and six years later constructed a refinery in East London. It produced Golden Syrup,

Buy your Sugar in sealed packets and obtain guaranteed quality with full net weight.

Uses for sugar suggested by the recently merged Tate & Lyle, 1920s.

a pale but flavourful liquid sweetener that was used for making preserves, as a sweetener in cooking and as a table syrup. The name Golden Syrup, trademarked in 1904, is believed to be the first British brand so registered. In 1921, these two companies consolidated to become Tate & Lyle, which remained one of Britain's largest sugar refiners until 2010, when it sold its refining operations to the American Refining Company.

Sugar beet was grown in Britain in the late nineteenth century, but the industry did not get off the ground until the First World War, when importing cane sugar became difficult. The industry thrived during the 1920s, but suffered during the Depression. In 1936, Britain nationalized the sugar beet industry and combined several companies into what became British Sugar. In 1991, British Sugar became a subsidiary of Associated British Food (ABF). Today, more sugar is refined in the UK from sugar beet than from imported sugar cane.

砂糖味甘寒無毒性冷利主心肺大腸熱

和中助脾殺蟲解酒毒多食損齒發疳

心痛生蟲消肌小兒尤忌同鯽魚食成

疳蟲同筍食筍不化成癥同葵菜食生

Granulated sugar (*shatang*) from *Shiwu bencao* (Materia dietetica), a herbal dating from the Ming period (1368–1644). Behind the man is a press for extracting sugar cane juice.

4
Sugar Uses

For much of sugar's history, the only way to taste it was to suck or chew on a cut stalk of sugar cane and enjoy the sweet juice. For at least the last 2,500 years, people in cane-growing areas have used that liquid and products made from it to sweeten foods and make alcoholic beverages. In ancient times on the Indian subcontinent, cane sugar was added to wine made from dates; fruit juice was sweetened with sugar; and sugar water, sometimes flavoured with herbs, was added to other beverages. The Indian epic *Mahābhārata*, which is attributed to Krishna-Dwaipayana Vyasa (*c.* 400 BCE), mentions sweets made with sugar and *krisara*, a liquid food consisting of five ingredients – milk, ground sesame seeds, rice, sugar and spices. The combination would survive, although with shifts in ingredients and consistency, to become punch (from *panch*, the Sanskrit word for five). At first, these foods and beverages were reserved for wealthy households and special celebrations. By the thirteenth century, however, sugar was plentiful enough in India to be widely available, even to the less prosperous in areas where sugar cane was grown.

By the 1200s, sugar was commonplace in southern and eastern China. The writer Wu Zimu describes, in his *Meng liang lu* (The Past Seems a Dream), seven confectionery shops in

Hangzhou in eastern China; they sold coloured, flower-shaped candies, sweet rice porridge, spun sugar, flavoured pastes, musk-flavoured sugar and preserved fruits in sugar syrup. Two Chinese cookbooks of the mid-thirteenth century have survived, and both include recipes for cakes, candies and syrups made with sugar-cane products. Sucheta Mazumdar, the author of *Sugar and Society in China* (1998), calculated that almost 17 per cent of the recipes in one book, and 25 per cent in the other, call for sugar. Both offer recipes for fruits and vegetables preserved in sugar. These were very useful formulas: abundant when in season, fruits and vegetables rot quickly after picking. Preserving them in sugar made it possible to enjoy them when fresh produce was unavailable. Sugar also masked the unpleasant flavours of unripe or overripe fruit. Sugared fruits and vegetables were popular throughout southern China, sold by street vendors and in teahouses and taverns.

Rock candy was made by boiling cane syrup to supersaturation point, then pouring it into moulds and drying it in the sun. There was also a paste of sugar and ground pine nuts (or walnuts) that could be pressed into moulds to create edible sculptures of flowers, animals, birds and fruit. The combination of sugar and ground nuts later evolved into the almond paste called marzipan, the emblematic sweet of the Middle East and Mediterranean.

Sugar cane arrived in the Middle East by the seventh century and quickly became a culinary sensation in Persia, Iraq and Egypt. Ibn Sayyar Al-Warraq's tenth-century Baghdadi cookbook includes more than 80 references to sugar in recipes for wine, sugared almonds and walnuts, cookies, crackers, pudding, chewy nougats and hard candies. Many of these recipes have survived in various forms. Al-Warraq's recipe for *natif*, or nougat, may well have been the inspiration for modern

Turkish Delight. Al-Warraq's book also included special recipes for the young, the elderly and travellers. For medicinal purposes, the author noted, sugar was soothing to the throat, chest and stomach, and had other important properties.

Small pies filled with sugar and sweetmeats were popular at this time; another very common treat was a thin pancake folded over several times, saturated with melted butter and sweetened with honey or sugar. Another was *kunáfeh*, thin, finely shredded dough moistened with clarified butter, doused with honey or sugar syrup and baked. It was in the Arab world that sugar began appearing in savoury dishes, such as lamb or mutton stewed with peaches, apricots and jujubes (the fruit of the tropical tree *Ziziphus jujuba*, sometimes called Chinese dates). Sugar was also used to sweeten beverages. The Arabs made a drink called *sharbah* by stirring a sugar syrup infused with rose petals, orange flowers, willow flowers or violets into cold water. Other *sharbahs* were made with raisins or fruit conserves. When ice was added to the mixture, it evolved into the frozen dessert that Europeans called sherbet.

Refined sugar achieved its pinnacle of conspicuous consumption in the households of wealthy Egyptians. According to Adam Mez, author of *Die Renaissance des Islams* (1922), the Vizier Qafur's household consumed 1,000 lb (450 kg) of sugar daily in 970 CE; during the following century, one Egyptian vizier's banquet featured 20 tons of sugar sculptures in the form of castles and various animals – elephants, lions and deer. Another feast was ornamented with 50,000 sugar figures, each weighing about 4 lb (1.8 kg).

European Sugar Usage

Prior to the ninth century, the small amounts of sugar that arrived in Europe were used for medical purposes. At that time, the humoral system, linking a person's health and temperament to different bodily fluids, had dominated European medical theories for more than a millennium and would continue to do so for almost another 1,000 years. In this system, 'sweetness' was a positive quality, and as sugar was the sweetest substance known, it was considered a sort of miracle drug. In addition to its own healing attributes, it could be combined with other medicines to make them more palatable, and sugar supplied calories – and therefore energy – to anyone who consumed it.

Beginning in the ninth century, Venice imported quantities of molasses, sugar and syrups from Egypt and the eastern Mediterranean. Sugar was re-exported from Venice to the rest of Europe. Northern Italian medical writings mentioned sugar in recipes and formulas beginning in the thirteenth century. For instance, *Tacuinum sanitatis* (Maintenance of Health), based on an eleventh-century Arab health manuscript, listed the pros and cons of sugar:

> It purifies the body, is good for the chest, the kidneys, and the bladder. Dangers: it causes thirst and moves bilious humours. Neutralization of the dangers: with sour pomegranates. Effects: Produces blood that is not bad. It is good for all temperaments, at all ages, in every season and region.

Venetian apothecaries specialized in refining raw sugar and became skilful in making syrups, jams, nut-paste confections, candied violets and a 'celestial water of youth', touted as an elixir for long life. Sugar was given as gifts and it was a must at marriage ceremonies, at which brides were given a box of sweets together with a sugar statuette of a baby.

As sugar became more common over the course of the fourteenth century, it appeared more frequently in cookery manuscripts. In the version of *Le Viandier* from 1300 (a later version of which was attributed to Guillaume Tirel – aka 'Taillevent'), sugar appears only in dishes for the sick. In a version of the same manuscript from 1420, sugar is used in most of the recipes. The early fourteenth-century cookery manuscript *Liber de coquina*, probably written in Naples, called for abundant use of honey, but occasionally replaced it with sugar; in such cases the sugar was mixed in with the other ingredients rather than poured over a finished dish, as honey was. Sugar was used in recipes for broad beans flavoured with spices; rice with almond milk; a *torta* sweetened with both sugar and honey; and a dish made with bitter oranges. A Tuscan recipe collection from the end of the fourteenth century emphasized sugar, giving only a marginal role to honey (in fritters and some desserts). Of the 135 recipes in the manuscript, sugar was an ingredient in 24 per cent, according to Alberto Capatti and Massimo Montanari's *Italian Cuisine: A Cultural History* (2003).

By the fifteenth century, sugar was commonplace in wealthy European households; it was used in sauces, pastry, and confections. Maestro Martino's *Libro de arte coquinaria* (The Art of Cooking), written about 1465, used sugar in great quantities. More than 50 recipes include sugar – custard pies, fish and poultry dishes, potages, a dish of broad (fava) beans, sugar-coated seeds, hot and cold beverages, pan-fried cheese, fritters, macaroni and lasagna, tortes, marzipan, blancmange and preserves. Bartolomeo Platina's *De honesta voluptate et valetudine* (Right Pleasure and Good Health), published in 1474, makes even more use of sugar, as does Bartolomeo Scappi's *Opera dell'arte del cucinare* (The Art and Craft of a Master Cook), published in 1570. As one recipe reported, sugar was 'an excellent accompaniment to everything'.

Sugar continued to be a symbol of opulence and a sign of wealth. When Henry III, king of France and Poland, visited the city-state of Venice in 1574, sugar was a major component in a banquet given in his honour. The napkins, tablecloths, plates, cutlery – everything on the table – were made of sugar. The setting also boasted 1,250 figures designed by the sculptor Jacopo Sansovino, including a queen on horseback between two tigers, with the coat of arms of France on one and Poland on the other, as well as sugar figures of animals, plants, fruit, kings, popes and saints.

By the early seventeenth century, sugar was widely available throughout much of continental Europe, and on the

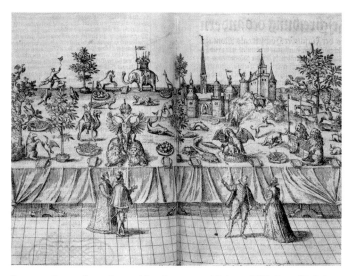

Sugar sculpture from the wedding banquet of Johann Wilhelm of Julich, Cleve & Berg, Dusseldorf, 1587.

tables of all but the poor. Naturally this robbed sugar of its cachet for the rich. The Florentine Giovanni Del Turco, in his *Epulario e segreti vari* (1602), complained that earlier cookbook writers had relied too heavily on spices and sugar, which did 'not appeal to the taste of many people'. The number of published recipes requiring sugar began to decline, and smaller quantities of it were used overall in sophisticated cookbooks.

English Sugar

In England, the account books of the household of Henry II (1154–1189) indicate that very small quantities of sugar were used. An entry in an account book from the Countess of Leicester's household records that 55 lb (25 kg) of sugar were acquired over a seven-month period in 1265, but the cost remained high. The English love affair with sugar – at least among the nobility – began in the fourteenth century. *The Forme of Cury* (*c.* 1390), written by Richard II's master cooks, includes numerous recipes with sugar as an ingredient: it went into fritters, custards, pies, sauces, stews, forcemeats, meat, fish, poultry, seafood and game recipes as well as alcoholic beverages, including Cypriot wine, German wine and mead. Within these recipes, sugar was combined with a wide variety of other ingredients, including currants, eggs, cheese, raisins, dates, milk, almond milk, figs, pears, rice, bread and virtually all the spices and herbs then available. Several recipes called for 'Cypriot sugar' as well as other types. Thereafter no feast or banquet was thought complete without sugar. The poem 'The Libelle of Englyshe Polycye', written about 1438, bemoans the importation of commodities from Florence and Venice, with one major exception – sugar:

'And yett. there shulde excepte be ony thynge, *It were but sugre*, truste to my seyinge.' The manuscript 'A Noble Boke off cookry' (*c.* 1480) contains scores of recipes with sugar, including those for beverages, such as one in which it is added to claret. In most cases sugar was used in small quantities and its sweetness did not dominate the recipe.

At most banquets, moreover, few sweet courses were served. This changed by the first decade of the sixteenth century, when the price of sugar dropped and it became affordable to households that were merely prosperous, not necessarily noble or royal. One of the poet Thomas Newbery's ballads mentions a confectioner's shop selling simnels (buns), cracknels (small cakes baked hard so that they crunched when broken), comfits (sweetmeats) and other products made with sugar. The price continued to drop throughout the century, and by the 1590s, sugar was the prime vehicle for demonstrating high status. The Earl of Hertford gave a banquet for Elizabeth I that included a vast display of decorative foods modelled in flat and three-dimensional sugarwork: 'March-paves, grapes, oisters, muscles, cockles, periwinkles, crabs, lobsters, Apples, pears, and plums of all sorts. Preserves, suckats, jellies, leaches, marmelats, pastry, comfits, of all sorts.' There were also:

> Castles, forts, Ordinance, Drummers, Trumpeters, and soldiers of all sorts in sugar-works. Lions, Unicorns, Bears, Horses, Camels, Bolls, Rams, Dogs, Tigers, Elephants, Antelopes, Dromadaries, Asses, and all other beasts in sugar-works. Eagles, Falcons, Cranes, Bustards, Herons, Hawks, Bitterns, Pheasants, Partridges, Quails, Larks, Sparrows, Pigeons, Cocks, owls, and all that fly, in sugar-works. Snakes, Adders, vipers, frogs, toads, and all kinds of worms, in sugar-work. Mermaids, whales, dolphins,

congars, sturgeons, pike, carp, bream, and all sorts of fishes, in sugar-work.

By the early seventeenth century, sugar was almost universally praised in Britain. Francis Bacon even proposed a statue for the 'Inventours of Sugars' in a gallery of important inventors in his utopian novel *Nova Atlantis* (1624). James Heart, author of *Klinke; or, the Diet of the Diseases* (1633), proclaimed that 'Sugar hath now succeeded honie, and is become of farre higher esteem, and is far more pleasing to the palate, and therefore everywhere in frequent use, as well in sickness as in health.'

The French-trained Gervase Markham, chef to England's aristocrats, offered dozens of recipes with sugar in *The English Hus-wife* (1615). These included salads, roasted meats, fish, sauces for turkey and other fowl, preserves, puddings, tarts, sweet and savoury pies, jumbles, cakes, pancakes, fritters, marchpane (marzipan), suckets and many more. The recipes in *The Queens Closet Opened* (1655) made prolific use of sugar. It was called for in preserves, cakes, cheesecakes, pancakes, bread, candy flowers, pumpkin and other pies, tarts, puddings, beans, preserves, salad dressings, alcoholic beverages (such as possets and syllabubs), creams and rudimentary forms of hard candy, as well as in medicinal formulas.

Toward the end of the seventeenth century, sugar lost some of its former charm for the British upper classes. Robert May's *The Accomplished Cook* (1685) mentioned sugar in only two recipes – sauces for meat and fish. John Evelyn's *Acetaria: A Discourse of Sallets* (1699) included a few dozen recipes with sugar in them, but he wrote that '*Sugar* is almost wholly banish'd from all, except the more effeminate Palates, as too much palling, and taking from the grateful *Acid* now in use, tho' otherwise not totally to be reproved.'

As the English upper classes became disenchanted with sugar, other strata of society discovered its allure, and its consumption surged. What fuelled its renewed popularity was beverages.

Drinking Sugar

Throughout the Middle Ages, the most popular European drink was hypocras or hippocras (probably named for the ancient Roman physician Hippocrates), a mulled or spiced wine commonly consumed at the end of a meal as a digestive. Traditionally hypocras was sweetened with honey. A late medieval French hypocras recipe attributed to the physician Arnoldus of Villanova (*c.* 1310) includes some sugar. In the Middle Ages, the French cookery manuscript *Le Ménagier de Paris* (*c.* 1393) includes a recipe containing 1¼ lb (570 g) of sugar. Recipes for hypocras continued to appear during the next three centuries. An English hypocras recipe from 1692 consisted of 2 quarts (1.9 litres) each of Rhine wine, Canary wine and milk, sweetened with 1½ lb (680 g) of sugar.

Hypocras disappeared in the eighteenth century, but by that time many other mixed drinks sweetened with sugar were popular. In England and America, these included flips (beer sweetened with sugar, molasses or honey, and frequently strengthened with rum) and possets (spiced, sweetened hot milk combined with ale or beer), which eventually evolved into eggnog. Syllabubs – spiced milk or cream whipped to a froth with sweet wine or cider and sugar – were spirituous drinks for festive occasions. Shrubs, composed of sweetened citrus juice from oranges, lemons and limes mixed with various spirits, were popular drinks, as were hot toddies, made of spiced and sweetened liquor, and cherry bounce, made from

Cachaça is a popular Brazilian rum-like beverage.

cherry juice and rum. There were iced punches for summer and hot punches for winter. Sangaree, a mixture of wine, sugar and spices, evolved into sangria.

European colonies in the New World produced different alcoholic beverages from sugar and its by-products. In Portuguese Brazil the sugar-based liquor was *cachaça*, a potent distilled alcoholic beverage. Portugal's large and politically powerful brandy industry squelched any possibility of competition from this imported product, so most *cachaça* remained in Brazil. But it was likely Dutch and Jewish immigrants from Brazil who introduced the concept of a sugar-cane-based spirit – and its means of manufacture – into the Caribbean. In the French West Indies it was called *rhum*, a word most likely derived from the English in Barbados, where it was variously called *kill-devil*, *rumme* and *rumbullion*. Eventually these terms were shortened simply to 'rum'.

Molasses, a by-product of sugar manufacturing, was also used to make mildly alcoholic beverages. West Indian slaves just added water to the molasses, which permitted fermentation. The early eighteenth-century historian Robert Beverley

Rum distillery in Christiansted, Saint Croix Island, Virgin Islands, 1941.

recorded that the 'poorer sort' of British colonists in Virginia used molasses to make a type of beer. It was often flavoured with bran, corn, persimmons, potatoes, pumpkins or even Jerusalem artichokes. In New England, molasses imported from the West Indies was used to make rum. New England was ideally suited for rum production: it had access to the metal and skilled workers needed to make the stills, an abundance of ships to transport the bulky molasses from the Caribbean, and plenty of wood for fuelling the stills and making barrels. Rum quickly became America's alcoholic beverage of choice. It was drunk straight, watered down or mixed with other ingredients – often including sugar. The most popular mixed drink was punch, usually composed of rum, citrus juice and sugar, with myriad variations. Milk punches, made with egg yolks, sugar, rum and nutmeg, were popular at parties and balls. Rum was quite popular in England, while in continental Europe the wine industry successfully fought for laws against its importation.

But it was in three non-alcoholic beverages – chocolate, coffee and tea – that sugar became indispensable throughout Europe, particularly England. The chocolate beverage originated in pre-Columbian Mexico, where it was made by mixing ground chocolate with water and flavouring it with vanilla, chilli peppers, achiote seeds and other ingredients. Since there were no sweeteners in the New World, it was an extremely bitter drink. European colonists, after tasting it, added other spices and sweetened it – at first with honey, and later with sugar.

Chocolate and the equipment needed to make it had been introduced into Spain from Central America in the early sixteenth century, but it was slow to catch on. From Spain, interest in chocolate spread to Italy, and from there to other European countries. At first, it was flavoured with a variety of New World ingredients and sweetened with honey. As the custom of drinking chocolate spread beyond the elite, sugar replaced honey. Among the earliest European recipes for cocoa is this one, dating from 1631, by the Spanish physician Antonio Colmenero de Ledesma, who wrote in the first treatise on chocolate:

> Take a hundred cacao kernels, two heads of Chili or long peppers, a handful of anise or orjevala, and two of mesachusil or vanilla – or, instead, six Alexandria roses, powdered – two drachms of cinnamon, a dozen almonds and as many hazelnuts, a half pound of white sugar, and annotto enough to color it, and you have the king of chocolates.

Over time, Europeans found that they preferred their chocolate without the exotic flavourings, but sugar remained in the mix. Hot chocolate did not become an important beverage in England until the second half of the seventeenth century: chocolate houses were established in London in the 1650s, and several publications extolled the drink's virtues and provided recipes for it. William Coles reported in his *Adam in Eden* (1657) that chocolate 'may be had in diverse places in London, at reasonable rates' and he added yet another benefit – it was, he claimed, an aphrodisiac. According to William Coles, chocolate had a 'wonderful efficacy for the procreation of children'. The first French recipe for hot chocolate appeared in Francois Massialot's *Le Cuisinier royal et bourgeois* (1693).

Coffee drinking originated in eastern Africa and the Arabian Peninsula. Beginning in the ninth century, it spread to the Middle East. Europeans visiting Turkey and Arab countries wrote about this new beverage, many complaining that it was too bitter. Some Egyptians added sugar to 'correct the bitterness', reported German botanist Johann Vesling, who visited Cairo in the 1630s. Turks opened the first coffeehouses in Europe in the mid-seventeenth century. The first coffee-house in Venice was established in 1629, and soon more opened in other major European cities. When coffeehouses first appeared in Europe, they served their coffee black, with sugar as an optional addition, but it soon became an inseparable companion to coffee.

About the same time that coffee and chocolate began to be appreciated in Europe, tea arrived from East Asia. Tea had been consumed in China for thousands of years, and by the Middle Ages tea leaves were exported from there by overland caravan via the Silk Road to the Middle East, and later to Russia. European explorers and travellers tasted tea while in East Asia, but it wasn't until the Dutch began importing it from China (by 1610) that tea became known in Western Europe. It arrived in England by the mid-seventeenth century, but at first was of interest only to the wealthy. By 1658, tea was being served in coffeehouses, and it quickly became popular. Samuel Pepys, a naval administrator who kept a diary record-ing the smallest details of his everyday life, reported that he drank his first cup of tea in 1660. Within a few years tea was sold in most London coffeehouses along with coffee, choc-olate and sherbet, a version of the Middle Eastern beverage made with flavoured sugar syrup.

Sugar was sometimes added to coffee, tea and chocolate in excessive amounts. In 1671, Philippe Dufour, a Parisian coffee seller, published *De l'usage du caphé, du thé, et du chocolate* (The Manner of Making of Coffee, Tea and Chocolate), which described how each of these beverages was consumed in 'Europe, Asia, Africa, and America'. Dufour recommended adding sugar to coffee, but he complained that some Parisians went overboard with this, until their coffee 'was nothing but a syrup of blackened water'.

The first coffeehouse in England was opened in 1652 by a Turkish merchant. A novelty became a trend and then a craze, and by 1675, London alone reportedly had more than 3,000 coffeehouses, frequented by the city's gentry and well-to-do merchants. While sipping their sweetened coffee, patrons discussed business affairs and politics.

Because of the high price of chocolate, coffee, tea and sugar, British coffeehouses remained the province of the well-to-do; lower classes gathered and drank beer in taverns. Then the British East India Company, a subsidized governmental monopoly, began to import tea in bulk: annual imports increased from 250,000 lb (113,000 kg) in 1725 to 24 million lb (10.9 million kg) in 1800. As volume increased, the price of tea fell below that of chocolate and coffee. Tea drinking soon outpaced the consumption of chocolate and coffee, and as more tea was imported, it became affordable for the middle class. Tea became England's hot beverage of choice.

During the eighteenth century, the sweetener of choice among the less affluent in England was honey, and for good reason: it was six to ten times cheaper than sugar. During the eighteenth century, sugar was imported from the English colonies in the Caribbean in ever-increasing quantities, and its price nosedived as consumption skyrocketed. At the beginning of the eighteenth century, annual per capita sugar consumption in England was 4.4 lb (2 kg) per person. In 1784, duties on imported tea were reduced, which was followed by a sharp increase in the use of tea. By the century's end, per capita sugar consumption had increased by almost 600 per cent, to 24 lb (10.9 kg). Even the poorest drank tea with sugar, though they could put little else on the table.

An Essential Ingredient in Cookery

Once the price of sugar dropped below that of honey, it began to be used not just as a sweetener for drinks, but as a cooking ingredient. English cookbooks published in the eighteenth century incorporated sugar into many recipes. Hannah Glasse published her *Complete Confectioner* in 1760 – the first such book published in England – and confidently called for sugar in almost every recipe. There were ice creams, ices, creams, conserves, compotes, marmalades, syrups, jams, cakes, icings, breads, biscuits, beverages, candies, wafers, jumbles, timbales, puffs and tarts, as well as directions for making sugar sculptures and preserving fruit, vegetables, berries, spices, nuts, seeds, roots and flowers. Elizabeth Raffald's *Experienced Housekeeper* (1769) contains more than 100 recipes containing sugar: sauces, pastes, pies, fritters, pancakes, gruels, puddings, dumplings, sweetmeats, custards, pastries, spun sugar, floating islands and all sorts of beverages – syllabubs, ales, various wines, possetts, sherbets, shrubs, brandy and lemonade. Sugar was no longer a luxury – it was an essential ingredient.

Just as sugar dominated English cookery, so it dominated American dishes, although refined sugar was expensive in colonial America. Far cheaper was molasses, which could be used both as a sweetener and as the basic ingredient in rum. Molasses was the primary sweetener for cookies, cakes, pies and puddings, but also in mush, vegetable dishes and meat cookery, especially pork. An English traveller in the 1780s complained that Americans served molasses at every meal, 'even eating it with greasy pork'.

Sugar was sold in many forms, the most common being 8- to 10-lb (3.6–4.5 kg) cone-shaped 'loaves'. The wealthy purchased large quantities of sugar, but a middle-class family might make one loaf last a year. It has been estimated that as late as

James Gillray, *Hero's recruiting at Kelsey's or Guard Day at St James's*, 1797, featuring ice cream.

1788, annual u.s. per capita sugar consumption averaged only about 5 lb (2.3 kg). Despite this rapid increase in the amount of sugar consumed throughout the world, the love affair with sugar had barely begun. The amount of sugar would increase in beverages, meats, pies and cakes, but particularly in sweets and candies.

5
Sweets and Candies

When sufficient sugar is added to certain foods, whether infused by cooking or applied as a coating, it functions as a preservative by inhibiting the activity of microorganisms. This quality made it possible for traders to carry products such as candied orange peel and sugar-coated almonds over long distances. Solid chunks of sugar (both rock candy and loaf sugar) could also easily be traded. It was through such trade that sweets and candies were introduced in areas where sugar cane was not grown, and where particular fruits and other ingredients were not available.

Through trade routes from southern Asia, sugar confections had reached the Middle East by the seventh century, later spreading to Europe. These early confections, such as comfits, pastes, marzipan, pastilles and rock candy, were the point of origin for many present-day sweets and candies, and traces of their centuries-old heritage still linger today. Early European confectionery traditions have evolved into modern sweets – Jordan almonds, marmalade, sweet pies, cake icing, taffy, toffee, bonbons, jawbreakers (gobstoppers), lemon drops, M&M's, Good & Plenty and ice cream – to name just a few.

Comfits (from the French *confit*, meaning 'candied' – *confetti* in Italian) were initially sugar-coated medicines. Doctors and other healers used the miraculously sweet substance to coat the bitter seeds, nuts, roots, spices, herbs and vegetable extracts they prescribed for various ills, doubtless helping the medicine go down. A sick person might need extra calories, which were easily supplied by sugar; depending on the number of comfits consumed, they may also have given a weak patient a little burst of energy.

Comfits that included candied aromatic seeds, such as anise, coriander, cloves, caraway or cinnamon, were common. In India (and in Indian restaurants elsewhere), plain or candy-coated fennel seeds may still be offered at the conclusion of a meal to aid digestion and freshen the breath. Comfits also included sugar-coated nuggets of candy flavoured with an extract from the roots of plants of the genus *Glycyrrhiza*, a small, leguminous shrub native to Europe, Asia and the Americas. The roots have a sweet, anise-like flavour, and a confection was made by squeezing their juice and then cooking it down to thicken it. Called 'liquorice', it became an important sweet throughout Europe from the Middle Ages onwards.

Today, liquorice candy is manufactured in many shapes and flavours throughout the world, although in many cases the actual root extract has been replaced with anise and artificial flavouring. In the United States, the most famous liquorice-flavoured candy is Good & Plenty – little beads of chewy liquorice with a pink or white candy coating reminiscent of traditional Indian comfits. It was first made in 1893. The artificially flavoured liquorice twists called Twizzlers were first sold in 1929. Today, most liquorice sold in the u.s. is mass-produced using synthetic ingredients, but elsewhere, notably in the Netherlands and Scandinavia, real liquorice in various shapes, hard or soft, from mildly sweet to pungently salty, is practically the national snack.

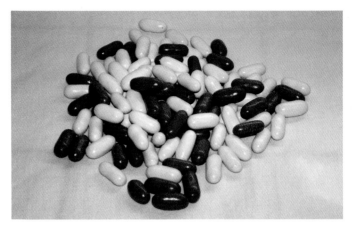

Good & Plenty liquorice candy, first made in 1893, remains popular today.

Another common comfit in the Middle Ages was the sugar-coated nut, which also originated in the Middle East and was later carried to Europe. The French term *dragées* describes spiced, sugar-covered nuts, especially almonds. Today, these have been commercialized under a variety of names, such as Jordan almonds, also known as *mlabas* in the Middle East and *koufeta* in Greece.

Candied fruit and citrus peel also arrived in Europe during the Middle Ages and were typically served after a meal at times of the year when fresh fruit was unavailable. They survive in a variety of forms – candied or glazed fruit, chocolate-dipped cherries, jams, marmalades and jellies.

Marzipan (or marchpane in English), a thick paste of ground almonds and sugar, was a popular delicacy in the Middle East by the Middle Ages. It may have originated in Iran, and arrived in Europe through Arab influence. The first located European reference to it is in northern Italy in the late thirteenth century. It's likely, however, that it had been a popular confection, probably made initially with honey,

Candied fruit at La Boqueria market in Barcelona.

in Spain, Catalonia and Italy well before that. Marzipan was widely adopted in France, Germany, the Netherlands, northern Europe and England. It wasn't just another bite-sized sweet – it was also shaped into figures, such as pigs or eggs, and was often given as gifts on special occasions, such as Christmas, Easter and at weddings. Marzipan remains popular in Europe and in many former European colonies.

Pulled sugar also arrived in Europe in the Middle Ages, likely from Arab sources in the Middle East. It is made by melting sugar with water, then kneading it to form a plastic substance that can be stretched and pulled into various shapes, such as ribbons, flowers or leaves.

During the Middle Ages sugar was also used as a post-prandial *digestif* – in sugared and spiced wine served with fruit at the end of the meal, after the dishes had been removed. This course came to be called dessert (from the French *desservir*, meaning to clear the table). By the eighteenth century, dessert had become an elaborate course that might include creams, jellies, tarts, pies and sweet puddings. Although typically served after dinner, such dishes could also be offered in the afternoon or evening, unconnected with a meal. Dessert-making became a household art, and was usually done by a professional confectioner or by servants under direction of a professional.

Bonbons, first made in France in the 17th century.

Meringue recipes have been published since the 18th century.

Laura Mason, in her book *Sugar-plums and Sherbet* (1998), writes that, by the eighteenth century, English confectioners sold preserved and candied fruit, biscuits, cakes, macaroons, syrups, comfits, pies, tarts and decorative figures made of sugar. Confectioners also imported and sold sweets from other countries. Bonbons (various types of fancy candies that were initially served at the French court) were imported into England and other European countries. These choice treats, consisting of fondant, fruit or nuts typically coated with chocolate, were a luxury for the leisure class – the only people who could afford them – but this was about to change.

Confectioners

By the seventeenth century, comfit-makers and confectioners were selling their sweets at shops for serving at home. Over time, retailers became more sophisticated. In Paris, *limonadiers* sold beverages such as lemonade (hence their name). One *limonadier*, a Sicilian named Francesco Procopio dei Coltelli, opened a café in Paris in 1686. In addition to serving coffee, the café also offered sugar-coated fruit, ices, sugar-sweetened cold beverages, liquors and hot chocolate.

Declining prices for sugar in the eighteenth and nineteenth centuries made sweets more affordable. In England, the number of sweet shops in provincial cities increased fourfold between the 1780s and the 1820s. They sold a variety of candies, some imported from other countries, some sent from London.

Particular types of sweets and candies emerged. Rock candy was made by allowing a supersaturated solution of sugar and water to crystallize over time; hard candies were made by boiling sugar and water to a syrup and then pouring it into moulds or shaping it by hand. These evolved into gobstoppers, lollipops, peppermints and candy canes. Sugared nuts were the

Rock candy has been made for about 2,000 years; it is still consumed today in different ways, such as on a stick.

starting point for brittles – whole or broken nuts embedded in a sheet of buttery hard candy. Fruit drops, originally made from boiled sugar flavoured with actual fruit juice, are still popular, although today many are made with corn syrup and artificial flavours and colourings that imitate the taste and appearance of fruit. Life Savers are the most famous modern incarnation of the fruit drop in the u.s. and Canada.

Taffy and Toffee

The first references to taffy and toffee appeared in the early nineteenth century in northern England, where the candy was made in homes and confectionery shops. (The candy-makers of Everton, today a district of Liverpool, were famous for their toffee.) The basic recipe calls for sugar or molasses to be boiled with butter and flavourings: orange, lemon, chocolate or vanilla. From this basic recipe, two different sweets emerged.

Taffy is made by removing the mixture from the fire at the 'hard ball' stage – when a drop of syrup instantly forms a rigid ball when dropped into cold water. The candy is cooled a little, then stretched and pulled by hand with the help of a metal hook until it is satiny smooth. In the nineteenth century, 'taffy-pulls' were popular at parties: guests would pair off to stretch the strands with buttered hands, and then enjoy the fruits of their labour.

To make toffee, the mixture is boiled to the 'hard crack' stage, at which a drop of the boiling syrup forms brittle threads when dropped into cold water. When cooled, this produces a dense candy that snaps when broken. In England, toffee was associated with Guy Fawkes Night (5 November, also known as 'Bonfire Night') and was sold under the name 'Bonfire Toffee'.

Joseph William Thornton opened his first confectionery shop in Sheffield in October 1911; among his more popular items was toffee.

Taffy and toffee migrated from England to the United States by the 1840s, and both were popularized in East Coast cities, particularly Philadelphia and Atlantic City. John Ross Edmiston, a Pennsylvanian, was probably the first to sell 'saltwater taffy', supposedly created when a storm brought seawater flooding into his Atlantic City candy shop. There was actually no difference in the recipes for regular taffy and saltwater taffy, but the name caught on. Others perfected its formula and expanded the product line by making the candy in a range of appealing pastel colours, various flavours and diverse shapes. By the 1920s, more than 450 companies, many in seaside resorts, were manufacturing saltwater taffy in America.

Manufacturers

Handmade sweets had been sold commercially in Europe and North America since the late eighteenth century, but they were not widely consumed until the nineteenth century, when the price of sugar declined and the technology of refining it had become more efficient. Sweets were first mass-produced in England in the 1850s, but manufacturing quickly spread to other countries. Sweets appeared in ever-larger quantities and in more varied shapes and sizes as the century progressed. By the late nineteenth century, hundreds of commercial manufacturers of confectionery were operating in the Middle East, Europe and North America. Most produced small, hard sweets, usually retailed in shops, where they were displayed in big glass jars and sold for pennies.

Soft and chewy candies were also mass-produced. One popular confection that derived from the Middle East was Turkish Delight, or *rahat loukoum* ('rest for the throat'), made from sugar (originally honey), a starch or gelling agent such as gum arabic, and flavouring, often rosewater or orange-flower water. Chopped nuts, such as almonds, pistachios or hazelnuts, or pieces of dried fruit, may be added. The cooked mixture is cooled in a pan and then cut into squares and dredged in icing (powdered) sugar. Its invention is attributed to a Turkish confectioner of the mid-eighteenth century. The popularity of this sweet grew throughout the Middle East and Europe, especially Great Britain, where a Turkish Delight chocolate bar, with a rose-flavoured filling enrobed in milk chocolate, has been made since 1914.

Jellybeans – small, bean-shaped sugar confections with a firm jelly centre and a hard outer coating – may have derived from Turkish Delight. They come in different colours with various associated fruit flavours. The earliest located reference to jellybeans in print appears in an advertisement dated 1886 from Illinois, where they were touted as a Christmas candy. Jellybeans were commonly sold from jars in sweet shops, or in vending machines. It was not until the 1930s that jellybeans were also marketed as an Easter candy, presumably because of their egg-like appearance.

Albert and Gustav Goelitz, German immigrants who opened a candy store in Belleville, Illinois, in 1869, could be called the forefathers of the modern jellybean. By the turn of the century the family business was specializing in buttercream candies, including candy corn, a three-coloured (yellow, white and orange) candy mimicking an enlarged corn kernel. In 1976, Goelitz descendants created the 'gourmet' jellybean, smaller than the standard size and featuring un-expected flavours such as pear, watermelon, root beer and buttered popcorn (reportedly the most popular flavour). They named the new product Jelly Bellies, and now offer 50 flavours, including cappuccino, chilli-mango and piña colada. Today, the company makes Bertie Bott's Every Flavour Beans, named after a product mentioned in J. K. Rowling's Harry Potter books, and Sports Beans, with added vitamin C and electrolytes.

Chewy sweets date back at least to the Middle Ages, where they were made in the Middle East. Among the first commer-cial chewy candies were jujubes, named for the juju gum (derived from a shrub of the *Ziziphus* species) that was the main ingredient. Today these fruit-flavoured pastilles are made from potato starch, gum and sugar or another sweetener. Another chewy candy, fruit- and vegetable-shaped jujyfruits, soon emerged. The gummy bear was developed in Germany during the 1920s. Animal-derived gelatin is the basic ingredi-ent in these colourful little figures. In 1982, the German candy company Haribo first marketed their 'gummi' candy in the United States. Trolli, another German manufacturer, intro-duced gummy worms during the 1980s and they have remained popular ever since. Swedish Fish, another gummy favourite imported from Sweden since the 1960s, are made without

Jellybeans are popular candies at Christmastime and Easter.

animal gelatin. Gummy candies are made in hundreds of shapes and flavours throughout the world.

Holiday Sweets

Many sweets and candies are associated with holidays, particularly Christmas, Chanukah, Easter, Halloween and Valentine's Day. In periods when sugar was rare and costly, the less affluent would have eaten sweets only on such special occasions.

The tradition of Christmas fruitcakes dates back to the Middle Ages. Historically, such cakes were sweetened with candied fruit stirred into the batter or dough; by the sixteenth century, sugar was a basic ingredient, and a sugary icing was a common addition. Particular traditions emerged in different areas, such as the British Christmas cake and the German *Stollen*.

Cultures that celebrate the twelve days of Christmas (from 25 December through to 6 January) have their own traditional cakes. Twelfth Night, or Epiphany, is also Three Kings' Day; in France, a *galette des roix* (kings' cake) is served. In Spain and Latin America, the traditional pastry is the ring-shaped *rosca de reyes* (kings' ring), lavishly decorated with candied fruit. Different kinds of 'kings' cakes' are served on Epiphany in many countries; a special king's cake is also a Mardi Gras speciality in some places.

Many different types of sweet, such as butterscotch, chocolate, lemon, creams, caramels, jellybeans and others, were popular at Christmastime in various times and places. It was not until the mid-nineteenth century that the candy cane – a red-and-white striped candy stick with a crook at the top – became part of American Christmas celebrations. The candy cane's invention is attributed to August Imgard of Wooster,

Ohio, who purportedly made and decorated Christmas trees with paper ornaments and candy canes. They were not an immediate commercial success, although people made candy canes at home on a small scale. They were tricky to make and, because of their fragility, difficult to ship. This changed in the 1950s, when candy cane machines automated production and packaging innovations made it possible for the candy to reach its destination unbroken. Candy giants including Mars, Hershey and Nestlé now make their own brands of candy cane.

Halloween (or All Hallows' Eve – the night before All Saints' Day) is observed, mainly in English-speaking countries, on the night of 31 October, when children dressed in costumes go from house to house asking for sweets. Since Halloween comes during the apple season in many countries, it has long been celebrated with candied, toffee or caramel apples. Home-made sweets, such as candied popcorn balls and taffy, gradually gave way to commercial candy, notably candy corn (tricoloured kernel-shaped sweets), which was introduced in the 1880s. Today, miniature boxes of popular candies and small, individually wrapped versions of favourite candy bars are specially packaged for Halloween distribution. This Americanized, candy-filled version of Halloween has recently been adopted in other countries.

Fertility symbols employed in pagan celebrations of spring – rabbits, eggs and chicks – were absorbed into Christian celebrations of Easter. Giving Easter eggs to poor children was a tradition that began in medieval Europe. Easter candy, though, is a relatively recent tradition that may have originated in Eastern Europe. The first located reference to chocolate Easter eggs dates to 1820 in Italy. During the 1930s, Easter sweets, such as jellybeans and chocolate bunnies, became part of the Easter basket tradition. The American candy manufacturer Just Born Company began to make three-dimensional marshmallow Easter chicks, called Peeps, in 1953. In 2012, Americans spent more than $2.3 billion on Easter candies, including 90 million chocolate bunnies, 700 million marshmallow Peeps and 16 billion jellybeans.

Chanukah, the eight-day Festival of Lights, celebrates a Jewish military victory over the Seleucid Empire in 164 BCE and the rededication of the Second Temple in Jerusalem. Chanukah is celebrated at home, with modest presents for children, one for each night. Small coins, or *gelt*, were the usual gift. In the 1920s, urban candymakers began promoting their wares as ideal Chanukah gifts. New York's Loft Candy Company, for instance, sold round, flat chocolates wrapped in gold foil to simulate coins. Brooklyn-based Barton's, founded in 1938, made kosher chocolates for both Chanukah and Passover.

Valentine's Day (14 February), purportedly celebrated in honour of a saint killed in Roman times, was a popular holiday in medieval Europe. Precisely when candy became a Valentine's Day tradition is unclear, but in 1860 the British confectioner Richard Cadbury introduced the first Valentine's Day chocolate box, and couples still exchange elaborately boxed chocolates on that day. In America, Sweetheart candies, little sugar hearts bearing brief romantic mottos, were made by the New England Confectionery Company in 1902. By the twenty-first century, NECCO was producing about eight billion Sweethearts each year – virtually all of them sold during the six weeks before Valentine's Day.

Chocolates

Hot chocolate was consumed with sugar in Europe and North America by the mid-seventeenth century, but chocolate was not sold as a sweet until the nineteenth century. In 1815, Coenraad Van Houten, a Dutchman, developed a process for defatting chocolate and then subjecting it to an alkalizing process. This set in motion a series of discoveries that eventually made possible the manufacture of powdered cocoa, which was achieved in 1828. Eventually this led to the large-scale manufacture of chocolate in both powder and solid form.

Handmade chocolates were produced in England by the mid-nineteenth century. One manufacturer was John Cadbury, a Quaker and a strong temperance advocate who thought that it was important to provide alternatives to alcohol. In 1831, Cadbury began manufacturing cocoa for drinking chocolate; by 1866, Cadbury was also producing eating chocolate – handmade bonbons, chocolate-covered nougat and other chocolate candies. Cadbury began to produce milk chocolate in 1897. Another important chocolate manufacturer was Joseph Storrs Fry, another British Quaker, who invented a process for combining cocoa powder, sugar and melted cocoa butter to produce a thin paste that could be shaped in a mould to make chocolate bars. Soon, J. S. Fry & Sons was the largest manufacturer of chocolates in the world. In 1919, Cadbury acquired J. S. Fry & Sons, although a few Cadbury chocolate bars still bear the name 'Fry's'.

Cadbury itself was acquired by Kraft Foods in 2010, but three years later, Kraft span off its sweets and snack food to a new company, Mondelēz International. Today, Mondelēz's bestselling confectionery brands are Cadbury's Dairy Milk, Milka chocolates and Trident gum. These rank sixth, fifth and third in global sales.

The grocers William Tuke and Sons of York, England, began to sell cocoa in 1785. In 1862, Henry Isaac Rowntree acquired the Tukes's cocoa business. In 1881, the company introduced Rowntree's Fruit Pastilles and in 1893, Rowntree's

Shopkeeper Miss Roud selling chocolate to pupils in the tuck shop at the Schoolboy's Exhibition at the Horticultural Hall, Westminster, London, 2 January 1926.

Fruit Gums. Four years later, Rowntree & Company was established. Like Cadbury, Rowntree innovated exceptional benefit programmes for employees, including dining and other facilities, workers' councils, a pension scheme, unemployment benefits and annual paid holidays.

In 1931, Rowntree began an aggressive development programme. One key to its success was the company's relationship with Forrest Mars, whose Mars Bar had been introduced in England in 1932. Until then, 'combination bars' (which had multiple ingredients such as chocolate, peanuts, caramel and so on) had not been popular in Britain. The Chocolate Crisp was launched in 1935 and renamed the Kit Kat two years later. The Rowntree company introduced Smarties in 1937. These colourful sugar-coated chocolate drops remain popular today in the United Kingdom, South Africa, Canada and

Australia. Nestlé acquired Rowntree in 1988; subsequently many new chocolates and sweets have been introduced under the Rowntree brand.

American Chocolate Makers

Milton Hershey was a manufacturer of caramel candies in Lancaster, Pennsylvania. In 1893, he visited Chicago's Columbian Exposition and was fascinated by the chocolate-making machinery exhibited by Lehmann & Company of Dresden, Germany. Hershey bought Lehmann's machinery at the Exposition and had it shipped to Lancaster. Then he hired two chocolate makers from Baker's Chocolate and began mass-producing chocolate candies. Up to this time, all American chocolate candies had been made by hand. The Hershey Chocolate Company, a small subsidiary of Hershey's caramel business, initially produced breakfast cocoa, sweet chocolate, baking chocolate and a variety of small candies, eventually coming out with the Hershey's Milk Chocolate bar about 1905 and Hershey's Kisses in 1907. While the Hershey Chocolate Company was successful from the start, it received a major boost during the First World War, when Hershey chocolate bars were given to American soldiers fighting in Europe. Many had never eaten a chocolate bar before, and when they returned after the war, the demand for Hershey's products surged. Recently, the Hershey Company has expanded its global presence through increased sales and acquisitions. Its Reese's chocolates rank first in the u.s. and fourth globally in sales.

In 1922, Frank Mars of Minneapolis founded the Mar-O-Bar Company. It initially sold a bar composed of caramel, nuts and chocolate. The next year, the company introduced

Kit Kat bars originated in England; today they are available throughout most of the world.

Reese's Pieces were featured in the mega-hit movie *ET*.

Forrest Mars introduced the Mars Bar into Britain in 1932.

the Milky Way bar and in 1930, Snickers, a peanut-flavoured nougat bar topped with nuts and caramel and coated with chocolate. It quickly became one of the most popular candy bars in America, a position it has held ever since.

Frank Mars's son, Forrest Mars, did not get along with his father, so with $50,000 in his pocket he moved to England and formed a new company, Mars, Ltd. In 1932, he introduced the Mars bar, a slightly sweeter version of the Milky Way. By 1939, the company was ranked as Britain's third-largest confectionery manufacturer. When the Second World War started in 1939, Forrest Mars returned to the United States, where he launched a new company with Bruce Murric, the son of the president of the Hershey Company. Because both of their last names started with M, they called their new company M&M. Their first product was a small milk-chocolate drop covered with a hard sugar shell, a small Smarties clone, which they named M&M's Chocolate Candies. The two companies,

Mars's Milky Way was one of the first popular combination candy bars.

Mars and M&M, were not merged until 1964. Mars, Inc. has continued to expand, both through acquisitions and by creating new products. As of 2011, Mars controls 15 per cent of the global candy market and is the world's largest confectionery manufacturer. Their Dove chocolates (Galaxy in the UK), Orbit and Extra globally rank fifth, eighth and ninth respectively. For decades, Mars' M&M's were the world's largest selling confection. Sales hit $3.49 billion in globally in 2012, but M&M's were dethroned by Mars' Snickers, which had worldwide sales of $3.57 billion and is now the largest selling confectionery item in the world.

Other Confectionery Manufacturers

In the 1860s, Henri Nestlé, a German-born pharmacist living in Switzerland, developed condensed milk and successfully marketed an infant formula made from milk and flour. He sold his company in 1874, but it retained his name. Henri Nestlé then worked with his friend Daniel Peter, a chocolatier, to help perfect the milk chocolate bar. Peter's chocolate, made with Nestlé condensed milk, quickly became one of Europe's best-known chocolate brands.

Ovaltine, a Swiss product created by a physician in 1904 to nourish seriously ill patients, was widely marketed during the following decades. A sugary, malted chocolate powder designed to be mixed with milk and drunk hot or cold, Ovaltine's healthful qualities, particularly added vitamins, were touted in its advertising. Ovaltine's success encouraged Nestlé to market its own milk modifier: Nestlé Quik (also called Nesquik), a sweetened chocolate drink powder. It was introduced in 1948, and its long sponsorship of children's television programming ensured its lasting popularity. Its product line was subsequently extended to include sugary syrups and cereals.

Top-selling candy sold in the United States.

Beerntsen's Confectionary, a historic old-fashioned candy store in Manitowoc, Wisconsin.

Chocolate bars are made and marketed throughout the developed world.

The First World War depressed Nestlé's sales, but after the war the company began to expand. By the late 1920s, chocolate was its second most important product. In 1929, Nestlé acquired Daniel Peter's company and entered into manufacturing powdered chocolate for making chocolate milk, premium chocolates and solid chocolate bars. After the Second World War, Nestlé began to grow rapidly, in part by acquiring other companies. In 1988, Nestlé acquired the Italian chocolate maker Perugina and the English chocolate maker Rowntree. Its Kit Kat bar ranks tenth in sales globally.

Another large confectionery manufacturer is Perfetti Van Melle Group, which was formed in 2001 and is headquartered in Milan, Italy. Its Mentos mints and chewy sweets rank eleventh in global sales today.

Tens of thousands of brands of assorted sweets are manufactured worldwide. Swedes consume more sweets than any other people in the world (annually 37 lb, or 16.8 kg, per capita). The Swiss consume more chocolate (annually 25 lb or 11.3 kg per capita). Americans eat less candy per capita, but spend more money – hitting $32 billion per year – and the amount is still increasing, even during the recent economic downturn. Worldwide sales of confectionery have also been increasing, and today are estimated at $150 billion annually.

6

American Bliss

In addition to candies and confections, sugar is added to a large number of other products sold throughout the world, including breakfast cereals, biscuits (cookies), doughnuts, ice cream and soft drinks. Sugar is also added to processed foods that were not traditionally sweet, and where its flavour may not be dominant. Hidden sugar can be found in canned soups and vegetables; breads, crackers and chips; frozen dinners; condiments (ketchup, chilli sauce and Worcestershire sauce) and salad dressings; peanut butter; baby foods and infant formula; pizza; hot dogs and lunch meat; pickles and cocktail snacks; flavoured yogurt; frozen foods; fruit juice, fruit coolers, 'energy' and sports drinks; and even pet foods. Sugars hide in processed foods under a variety of names, including sucrose, glucose, dextrose, maltose, lactose, galactose, malt syrup, maltodextrin, corn syrup, high fructose corn syrup, molasses and corn sweetener, to name a few.

Nowhere is this sugarization of processed foods more apparent than in the United States. As sugar prices declined in the nineteenth century, sweet desserts and snacks became universal in American homes, regardless of income or social class. More and more sugar went into cakes, cookies, pies and other pastries. Foreign visitors remarked upon this, noting that

Cotton candy (candy floss), spun sugar in a paper cone, became popular in America in the early 20th century.

the amount of sugar and other sweeteners 'used in families, otherwise plain and frugal, was astonishing'. By the 1870s, U.S. sugar consumption per capita was 41 lb (18.6 kg) per year; as commercially processed foods came on the market and sugar prices sank further, American consumption shot up. Cakes, from simple to lavish, were becoming an everyday part of the American diet. Parties were celebrated with a profusion of jelly cakes, pound cakes, plum cakes and lady cakes. From American kitchens issued a steady, fragrant stream of sugar cookies, wafers, kisses, drops, jumbles, snaps, macaroons, gingerbread, crullers and doughnuts – all with ever-greater quantities of sugar. Sweet rolls and doughnuts became regular breakfast fare. By 1901, Americans were consuming an average 61 lb (27.7 kg) of sugar per capita per year. The American love affair with sugar was flourishing, but was still a long way from its peak.

Breakfast Cereal

Until the twentieth century, the typical American breakfast included fruit, breadstuffs, eggs, potatoes and meats of all kinds – not just bacon or sausage but beefsteak, savoury meat pies and calves' liver. During the late nineteenth century, vegetarians and health reformers began to develop breakfast foods based on unrefined whole grains, which they thought better suited to the digestion of the modern-day office worker. The first commercial cereals were unsweetened and were meant to be moistened with plain water. As the industry took off, entrepreneurs found that customers preferred their cereal sweeter, so the new fashion was to serve it with cream and sugar. Will Kellogg added sugar to the formula for Corn Flakes over the objections of his brother, the health food guru and vegetarian John Harvey Kellogg, who believed that ingesting sugar carried more potential health risks than eating meat.

As more women entered the workforce during the twentieth century, cereals were advertised as a means of easing mother's workload. Children could prepare their own breakfasts without help and they loved sugary cereal. According to the medical authorities of the day, cereal was good for children, so this was a double win for busy mothers. Cereal companies, largely because they aimed their marketing directly at children, did well during the Depression; adding more and more sugar to their products helped seal the deal. After the Second World War, with sugar rationing a thing of the past, cereal makers upped the ante even further. In 1949, Post Cereals introduced Sugar Crisp, puffed wheat with a crunchy sugar coating. It was an immediate success, and other cereal companies followed suit with heavily sweetened cereals targeted at children. Some cereals approached 50 per cent sugar by weight; Kellogg's Honey Smacks hit 55.6 per cent sugar; Post responded with

Super Orange Crisps, which weighed in at 70 per cent sugar. This led observers to ask, 'Is it cereal or candy?'

These high-sugar cereals were heavily promoted in children's media, especially radio and television, point-of-sale marketing and, later, the Internet. The big three American cereal manufacturers (Kellogg's, Quaker Oats and Post) spent more on advertising their products then they did on the ingredients that went into them. Annually the u.s. cereal industry uses 816 million lb of sugar, or almost 3 lb (1.4 kg) of sugar per capita. Ironically cold breakfast cereals, which started out as health foods, are now considered major contributors to excess sugar in the American diet, especially those of children. More than 1.3 million cereal commercials air on American television each year, and most of them are aimed at children.

Diverse breakfast cereals are numerous in American supermarkets.

Biscuits, Cookies, Cakes and Bread

The English word *biscuit* comes from Latin via Middle French; its original meaning was 'twice baked'. Some early European recipes (like those still used for Italian *biscotti*) called for dough to be baked in loaf form, then sliced or split and baked again, slowly, to drive off any moisture; the drier the product, the longer it would keep. British biscuit recipes came to America with the English colonists, but the Dutch also colonized parts of America and their word *koekje*, meaning small cake, became the American term for a sweet biscuit. Amelia Simmons, author of *American Cookery* (1796), is credited with publishing the first known 'cookie' recipes, including one for 'Christmas Cookeys' made with a pound and a half of sugar to three of flour.

Cookies are the simplest of baked goods and require few ingredients – sugar being one of them. They take only a few minutes in the oven, so they can be baked on short notice and served as an informal dessert or eaten as a snack. A full cookie jar was long seen as emblematic of a well-run American home, a loving mother and a happy family, and the cookies in the jar should be (it went without saying) home-baked: sugar-cookie cutouts, oatmeal or peanut-butter cookies or the classic chocolate-chip cookies. But neighbourhood bakeries and pastry shops offered more elaborate cookies, and commercial baking plants in the u.s. started to churn out mass-produced cookies in the nineteenth century. By the turn of the twentieth century, store-bought cookies were available nationwide, and advertising campaigns strove to make them acceptable to the fashionable hostess. The National Biscuit Company (later Nabisco), founded in 1898 as a conglomerate of smaller baking companies, pioneered a wide variety of cookies, such as Oreos, today the world's largest-selling cookie.

Christmas biscuits (cookies) have been served in Europe since the 16th century; they remain a Christmas treat today.

Cakes as we know them today began as a variation on breads. Some, like pancakes, were flat, and were turned to cook on both sides on a hot surface. Other cakes were baked in specially designed cake pans. If early cakes were sweetened, it was with a little honey, or they might be baked unsweetened and served with honey as an accompaniment. During the sixteenth and seventeenth centuries, sugar replaced honey in cake batters, and sugar-based icings or frostings supplanted the accompanying honey. By 1615, cookbooks were advising the use of 'a good deale of sugar' in cake recipes. By the 1680s, cakes were commonly served as a dessert after a meal, or with tea or coffee in the morning or afternoon. Lavishly decorated cakes became a feature of special occasions and ceremonial feasts, such as Christmas, weddings and birthdays. As sugar prices declined and sugar refining improved, the amount of refined sugar used in cakes increased; powdered or icing sugar (also called confectioners' sugar because it was used in candy-making) became widely available in the nineteenth century, when it began to be called for in recipes for cake icing.

Cake-baking traditions were brought to America by European immigrants, and cakes were popular in colonial times; they remain one of America's favourite desserts. From simple gingerbread, pound, angel food and sponge cake to rich fruitcakes, cheesecakes, frosted and filled layer cakes, elaborate wedding cakes and whimsically decorated cupcakes, American cakes call for generous amounts of sugar. Although many people still bake cakes from scratch at home – especially birthday cakes – there is an abundance of mixes, bakery cakes and packaged or frozen products for those not so inclined.

Historically bread was made without the addition of sugar, although some early nineteenth-century recipes published for brown bread (also called dyspepsia bread) included molasses. This changed when millstones in flour mills were replaced by high-speed steel rollers during the late nineteenth century. The bran, germ and oil were removed from the wheat to produce a bland white flour. Bakers began to compensate for this tastelessness by adding sugar, and the amount of added sugar increased over time (sugar also adds moisture to bread, so it stays fresh longer). In the 1880s, cookbook authors recommended one tablespoon of sugar to every eight cups of flour. By the 1890s, this had increased in some recipes to about one tablespoon per cup of flour. Commercial bakers added even more. This increased even more for commercial bread during the twentieth century. By comparison, bakers in other countries, such as Italy and France, include little or no sugar in their bread.

Doughnuts

American doughnuts (or donuts) may have been of Dutch, German or English origin. The Dutch called them *olijkoeken* (oil cakes) or *oliebollen*. These were pinched-off portions of sweetened dough that were rolled between the hands and then dropped into hot oil. The Dutch-style nuggets or 'nuts' of fried dough were popular in America, but doughnuts with holes in the centre were not common until the end of the nineteenth century. Purportedly the hole was a practical innovation that made for easier dunking in coffee. Others maintain that the shape helped the dough to cook more evenly.

The sale of commercial doughnuts greatly expanded after the Second World War. Doughnut retailing lends itself to franchising because the equipment is affordable. Doughnut franchisers include Dunkin' Donuts, House of Donuts, Krispy Kreme and Winchell's. Dunkin' Donuts alone sells an estimated 6.4 million doughnuts per day (2.3 billion per year).

Yet another doughnut chain was established by Tim Horton, a hall-of-fame Canadian hockey player, who opened his first outlet in Hamilton, Ontario, in 1964. It was known for its coffee, which was guaranteed to be served fresh, cappuccinos, doughnuts and 'donut holes', but it quickly incorporated other items. The company soon expanded and it became Canada's largest fast food operation. In 1995, Tim Hortons opened outlets in the United States. When Burger King agreed to purchase the chain in 2014, Tim Hortons had almost 4,600 systemwide restaurants, inluding about 845 in the United States and other countries.

About 80 per cent of doughnut business is take-out, and 80 per cent of doughnuts are sold before noon in North America. They come in a great diversity of shapes, sizes and flavours. There are yeast-raised doughnuts and baking-powder

Entenmann's doughnut variety pack.

doughnuts, both deep-fried; for the fat-avoidant, oven-baked doughnuts are available. Most doughnuts have holes, and doughnut holes (or pieces of dough shaped to resemble them) are sold separately. Filled doughnuts are injected with jam (jelly), custard or a variety of other sweet fillings; further adornments may include a thick dusting of icing (confectioners') sugar or cinnamon sugar, a thin layer of chocolate icing, a vanilla, chocolate or other flavour glaze, toasted coconut or sprinkles. Similar pastries are crullers (or krullers), large strips of dough twisted together and fried; and bismarcks, large, éclair-shaped jam doughnuts.

Ice Cream

Ices, ice creams, and sorbets – frozen desserts initially sweetened with fruit juice – likely originated in Italy or France in the sixteenth century. They were sold in cafés in Europe from the seventeenth century on, and small vendors operated in most European cities by the 1800s. Several ice-cream recipes appeared in English cookbooks in the eighteenth century. European immigrants brought ice-cream-making techniques to America, where ice-cream parlours had opened in some cities by the 1790s. Many ice-cream recipes – most sweetened with plenty of sugar – appear in nineteenth-century American cookbooks.

Three main ice-cream flavours – chocolate, vanilla and strawberry – came to the fore in the nineteenth century and have remained favourites ever since. But other flavours proliferated during the nineteenth century, as did elaborate ice-cream presentations with inventive toppings, sauces and garnishes, and soda-fountain drinks made with ice cream. The late twentieth century saw the rise of the mix-in – premium ice cream studded with chunks of cookies, candies, chocolate, nuts or fruit, or with thick swirls of caramel, fudge or peanut butter running through the cream.

For much of the nineteenth century, going out for ice cream was a genteel pursuit. Served in establishments called 'parlours', ice cream was scooped into elegant glass dishes and eaten with a spoon. It was a popular summer treat, and the ingredients were cheap, but the problems for street vendors were how to keep the product cold and how to serve it without dishes and spoons. The solution was the ice cream cone, which was invented in the late nineteenth century.

Commercial production of ice cream did not take hold until technological improvements in refrigeration made sales possible through drugstores, soda fountains and grocery stores. In the United States, soda fountain offerings competed with the alcohol served in saloons and bars, and were therefore championed by the temperance movement. Prohibition gave a huge boost to the popularity of ice cream as bars, saloons and taverns were shuttered and soda fountains became community gathering places. However, it was not until after the Second World War, when self-serve freezer chests for grocery stores came into wide use and the freezer sections of home refrigerators increased in size and efficiency, that packaged ice cream became an everyday part of the diet.

By the 1950s, large ice-cream makers were underselling small producers, and supermarkets switched to national brands. But a niche had opened up for 'super-premium' ice creams, with a higher butterfat content and less air than supermarket brands. Häagen-Dazs, a new product from a decades-old family ice-cream business, first appeared in 1960, and Ben & Jerry's ice cream, originally made by hand by two young men from Long Island, was first sold from a converted gas station in Burlington, Vermont, in 1978. Breyers is still the largest ice-cream manufacturer in America, a position it has held since 1951. It is followed by Dreyer's/Edy's and Blue Bell Creameries, Inc. Despite the concentration of the ice cream industry, the largest category of ice-cream makers in America today is private labels, generally sold at the local and regional level. In 2013, Americans purchased an estimated $11 billion worth of ice-cream – complete with a generous helping of sugar in virtually every serving.

Sugary Beverages

Yet another sugar-filled treat is soda pop, which, like breakfast cereal, began life as a health food and ended up as just the opposite. Mineral waters, both still and naturally effervescent, have long been considered therapeutic, and water artificially infused with carbon dioxide (CO_2) was considered to have medicinal attributes. At European spas and resorts built at natural springs, drinking bubbly mineral waters was an important part of the health regimen. During the eighteenth century, several scientists, including Joseph Priestley and Antoine-Laurent Lavoisier, discovered that carbon dioxide was the source of the bubbles in natural springs, beer and champagne. Priestley constructed an apparatus for manufacturing the gas, and reports of his invention were sent to John Montagu, the fourth Earl of Sandwich (the same man credited with inventing the sandwich), who was then Lord of the Admiralty. He requested that Priestley demonstrate his apparatus before the Royal College of Physicians. Priestley did so; among the audience members was Benjamin Franklin, who was living in London at the time.

Other scientists constructed their own systems for producing soda water. In 1783, Johann Jacob Schweppe improved a process for manufacturing carbonated water and formed the Schweppes Company in Geneva, Switzerland. During the French Revolution and its aftermath, Schweppes moved his operation to England, where his soda water was approved for medicinal use by the British royal family.

By 1800, manufacturers had found they could make water fizzy by adding a solution of sodium bicarbonate to it. Carbonated water, however, was generally made under high pressure using sulphuric acid. Operators could easily be burned by the acid, and containers sometimes exploded. Various kinds of apparatus for making carbonated water were patented from 1810, but because of the complexity of the process, they could be operated only by trained technicians. Because the devices were expensive, and the beverages made with them were considered medicinal, soda water was generally dispensed only in drugstores. It was a small step from carbonated water to flavoured soda water. Ginger ale is generally thought to have been the first flavoured carbonated beverage sold commercially in America. It was probably first marketed in 1866 by

James Vernor, a Detroit pharmacist, who created Vernors Ginger Ale.

Another early soft drink was root beer, which was traditionally flavoured with bark, leaves, roots, herbs, spices and other aromatic parts of plants. In its early years, root beer was a home-brewed, mildly alcoholic beverage. Later, extracts made from the flavourful ingredients were touted as a tonic – typical of herbal remedies of the period. By the 1840s, root beer mixes and syrups were manufactured locally and sold in confectionery and general stores. Soda fountains, which sold combinations of ice cream and drinks composed of fruit syrups, sugar and soda water, sprang up around America.

Soda companies produced a sugary syrup or extract and sold it to drugstores, where it would be combined with carbonated water. This began to change in 1892, when William Painter invented the crown bottle cap, which made it possible to seal bottles easily, cheaply and securely. At the same time, bottling technology improved: the new, stronger glass bottles could hold the 'fizz' without shattering during bottling.

Soft drinks got another major boost during Prohibition, when manufacturing and selling alcoholic beverages was illegal. It was also during the 1920s that fast food chains emerged, and virtually all of them sold soft drinks. When Prohibition was repealed in 1933, soft drinks and fast food outlets were already well-established American institutions and they continued on their upward sales trajectory.

Soft drink manufacturers spend billions of dollars on promotion and advertising. Marketing efforts are aimed at children through cartoons, movies, videos, charities and amusement parks. In addition, soft drink companies sponsor contests, sweepstakes and games via broadcast and print media as well as the Internet, much of it targeting young people. In its study *Liquid Candy* of 2005, the Center for Science in the Public

Interest (CSPI) revealed that soft drink companies had targeted schools for their advertising and sales of their products. It also reported that soft drinks 'provided more than one-third of all refined sugars in the diet'. Soft drinks, according to CSPI, are the single greatest source of refined sugar, providing 9 per cent of calories for boys and 8 per cent for girls. The CSPI study also reported that at least 75 per cent of American teenagers drink soda every day.

American soda companies have rapidly expanded abroad. Coca-Cola and PepsiCo sell more than 70 per cent of the carbonated beverages in the world. Worldwide, soda companies sell the equivalent of 1.3 billion glasses of soda every day, which works out to about eight teaspoons of sugar per glass of non-diet soda.

Energy and Sports Drinks

Added sugar is also found in many other beverages, including fruit juices, fruit coolers, coffee beverages and 'energy drinks'. Sugar has been added to fruit drinks ever since they emerged as a mass-consumption processed product in the 1940s.

Manufacturers have used the word 'fruit' in their beverage names to persuade potential buyers of good nutrition inside the can or bottle, but many fruit drinks are just fruit-flavoured sugar water. Fruit coolers, for instance, typically have 16 grams of sugar. Other beverages have more. A 20 oz (600 ml) bottle of Vitamin Water contains 33 grams of sugar. A 16 oz (475 ml) Starbucks Café Vanilla Frappuccino has 67 grams per serving. A Costa Medio Tropical Fruit Cooler contains 73 grams of sugar – seven times more than a Krispy Kreme doughnut.

Energy drinks have become pervasive and most are filled with sweeteners. An English pharmaceutical company developed the first energy drink, called Glucozade, in 1927. It was a fizzy liquid filled with sugar, and was mainly used to help children recover from illness. A British pharmaceutical picked up the formula, renamed it Lucozade, and promoted it with the slogan 'Lucozade aids recovery.' In 1983, the company decided to reposition the product as an energy drink using the slogan, 'Lucozade replaces lost energy.'

Red Bull, consisting of caffeine, sucrose, glucose and other ingredients, was launched in Europe in 1987. It was introduced into the United States a decade later, when it became America's first popular energy drink. Red Bull started a frenzy of copycat beverages, such as Jolt, Monster Energy, No Fear, Rockstar, Full Throttle and a myriad of other brands. Large companies jumped in: Anheuser-Busch's 180, Coca-Cola's KMX, Del Monte Foods' Bloom Energy and PepsiCo's Adrenaline Rush. These drinks boast caffeine levels of up to 500 mg per 16 oz (475 ml), and they are often loaded with various forms of sugar. By the early twenty-first century there were more than 300 branded energy drinks on the market in America alone – and most were filled with high-calorie sweeteners.

Sugar is also a major ingredient in many sports drinks – beverages that are designed to enhance athletic performance by fostering endurance and recovery. The first such beverage was Gatorade, formulated in 1965 by Robert Cade and Dana Shires of the University of Florida. Gatorade is a noncarbonated drink that consists of water, electrolytes and a heavy dose of carbohydrates (in this case, mainly sugar – 28 grams of which are in 16 oz of the drink). Gatorade launched the sports-beverage industry. Intended for athletes participating in serious competition or intense exercise, sports drinks do increase energy levels (as do all sugar-sweetened drinks) – but most sports and energy drinks are consumed by non-athletes, who often end up gaining weight.

Bliss Point

That sweetened products sell well has been known since the early twentieth century. Manufacturers wanted to know how much sugar should be added for maximum sales. The research started in the early 1970s, when the psychologists Anthony Sclafani and Deleri Springer engaged in an experiment to induce obesity in laboratory rats. They found that rats did not overeat or gain weight when they were fed only Purina Dog Chow, but became obese when given Froot Loops, a high-sugar breakfast cereal. Sclafani and Springer repeated their experiment using other common supermarket foods – peanut butter, marshmallows, chocolate bars, sweetened condensed milk and chocolate-chip cookies. The rats preferred sweet food – and, if given the opportunity, continued to eat it until they became obese. Other experiments subsequently proved that when obese rats were exposed to non-sweet standard rat food, they declined to eat it.

About the same time, Howard Moskowitz, a researcher in the u.s. Army labs in Natick, Massachusetts, was searching for ways to make military rations more palatable for soldiers in combat. His experiments showed that soldiers' preferences for foods increased as sugar was added – up to a point – but beyond that point, additional sugar made the food *less* appealing. Moskowitz is credited with coining the term 'bliss point' to describe that peak in the appeal of sweetness (bliss points were also established for fat and salt intake). The conclusion of these and other studies was that a love for sugar was inborn, and that humans were hardwired to prefer sweet foods. In 1981, Moskowitz left the Army labs and opened his own consulting firm in White Plains, New York, where many American food companies were headquartered. His company helped food corporations find the 'bliss point' for their products. He was extremely successful and so were the companies he advised.

Yet another set of experiments was conducted at the Monell Chemical Senses Center in Philadelphia, an independent non-profit research facility funded by governmental agencies and large corporations. Researchers concluded that children, in particular, preferred sweeter foods than adults. Later experiments at the Center found that a preference for sweet flavours was a basic part of children's biology, and allowed researchers to determine the exact bliss point for sugar in children's foods and beverages. Further studies around the world, such as at the London-based – and corporate-funded – ARISE (Associates for Research into the Science of Enjoyment), confirmed these studies and concluded that the taste for sweetness was inborn.

These studies helped food manufacturers figure out how much sugar to incorporate in their products in order to stimulate sales. Candy and cereal companies, bakers and soft-drink manufacturers throughout the world raised the levels of sweetness in their products to the scientifically identified bliss point. The consumption of sugary foods and beverages rapidly expanded – as did the waistlines of consumers around the world, generating considerable criticism for the processed and fast food industries.

7
Sugar Blues

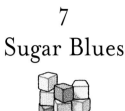

Concerns about the health effects of consuming sugar have been expressed for the past four centuries. The main early concern was the relationship between sugar consumption and dental caries (cavities). One of the first references to this is in the writings of Paul Hentzner, a German visitor to England who met the 66-year-old Elizabeth I in 1598. He described her as having black teeth, commenting that it was 'a defect the English seem subject to from their too great use of sugar'. The medical authorities agreed: sugar rotted the teeth. William Vaughan, a doctor of civil law, condemned sugar for various reasons; one, as he wrote in his work *Approved Directions for Health* (1612), was that it blackened and 'corrupted' teeth. James Hart, author of *Klinike; or, the Diet of the Diseases* (1633), proclaimed that the immoderate use of sugar in sugar candy, sweet confections and sugar-plums produced 'dangerous effect in the body,' including constipation, consumption, blockages and 'rotten teeth, making them look blacke'. He went on to warn 'young people especially to beware' of consuming these confections. Writers continued to note the relationship for centuries. Jonathan Swift, for instance, proclaimed that 'sweet things are bad for the teeth' in one of the dialogues in *A Complete Collection of Polite and Ingenious Conversation* (1722).

Colour lithograph after Reginald Mount, and issued by the Ministry of Health, 1950s.

American medical authorities later expressed their own concerns about refined sugar. The health advocate Sylvester Graham, in his final work, *Lectures on the Science of Human Life* (1839), advocated banning refined sugar because it was stimulating: 'The stern truth is, that no purely stimulating substances of any kind can be habitually used by man, without injury to the whole nature.' Many health reformers followed Graham's beliefs. The hydropath Russell Trall violently attacked sugar in editorials and in his books on health:

> Sugar is made into an immense variety of candies, confections, lozenges, etc., most of which are poisoned with coloring matters, and many of which are drugged with apothecary stuff. The intelligent physiologist will repudiate their employment in every form or shape. The raw sugars of commerce contain various impurities; and the refined and very dry sugars tend to constipate the bowels.

Not all health reformers heeded Trall's absolutist views on sugar. John Harvey Kellogg, the Seventh-Day Adventist who directed the sanatorium in Battle Creek, Michigan, felt that his childhood gastrointestinal problems were caused by meat and candy, and believed that the American love of candy and sweet desserts needed to be rigidly controlled, for sugar interfered with proper digestion. But he did not call for the complete elimination of sugar, recommending only that people should eat much less of it, and replace it with honey, dates and raisins.

Dentists, understandably, condemned sugar, but medical authorities were also concerned. In 1942, the American Medical Association's Council on Food and Nutrition stated that 'it would be in the interest of the public health for all practical means to be taken to limit consumption of sugar in any form in which it fails to be combined with significant proportions of other foods of high nutritive quality.' The medical profession also worried about sugar consumption, particularly its effects on hypoglycaemia (low levels of sugar in the blood). E. M. Abrahamson, MD, and A. W. Pezet, in their book *Body, Mind, and Sugar* (1951), concluded that refined sugar caused a 'constellation of diseases', and that its removal from the diet led to immediate improvement in patients' health. The book was mainly based on personal experiences – Abrahamson was a physician specializing in diabetes who dosed Pezet with 'hyperinsulinism' – but it received wide publicity and sold more than 200,000 copies. Other medical professionals agreed. A British Royal Navy surgeon, Thomas L. Cleave, and a South African physician, George D. Campbell, examined a number of different societies and found that diabetes, heart disease, obesity, peptic ulcers and other chronic diseases were correlated with increased consumption of refined sugar, white flour and white rice. The less refined carbohydrates that were consumed, the lower the incidence of these diseases. They published their views in the book *Diabetes, Coronary Thrombosis and the Saccharine Diseases* (1966). While their beliefs were scoffed at by some, most medical professionals did recommend that their patients reduce their intake of added sugar.

Sugar Substitutes

Concern with increasing diabetes and obesity led to the invention of non-caloric and low-calorie artificial sweeteners. The first artificial sweetener was saccharin, a white crystalline powder that has 300 to 500 times the sweetness of sugar, but no calories. It was discovered by a graduate student at Johns Hopkins University in Baltimore in 1879. Saccharin was commercialized by several companies, including Monsanto, but was not widely used until sugar rationing was encouraged during the First World War.

After the war, saccharin became a boon to diabetics, and eventually was used in diet products for weight-loss regimes.

Broadside encouraging Americans to consume less sugar during the First World War.

In 1977, a Canadian study reported that saccharin caused cancer in test animals, and the U.S. Food and Drug Administration (FDA) placed a moratorium on its use until more studies were conducted. Further studies did not confirm earlier test results and the ban was lifted in 1991.

A second artificial sweetener, calcium cyclamate, was used in diet soda beginning in 1952. Variations of it were used in a variety of other products. Lab studies carried out in the late 1960s showed that cyclamates were likely carcinogenic, and they were banned by the FDA in 1970. By the late 1970s, most diet products were being made with a third sugar substitute, aspartame (marketed under the names NutraSweet and Equal).

Stevia is a non-caloric natural sugar substitute derived from plants in the sunflower family. The plant extract is 300 times as sweet as table sugar. Stevia became popular in Japan in the 1970s and since then has been widely used in many countries in Asia and South America. In 1994, the FDA classified stevia as a herbal supplement and required it to be listed on the food labels. In 2008, the FDA approved two sweeteners derived from stevia: Truvia, developed by Cargill and the Coca-Cola Co., and PureVia, developed by PepsiCo and the Whole Earth Sweetener Company. The following year, the FDA placed a purified form of stevia on the 'Generally Recognized as Safe' list.

Another recent introduction is Sucralose, which is 600 times sweeter than table sugar. It was approved for use in Canada in 1991, and seven years later in the U.S. Marketed under several brand names – Splenda, SucraPlus, Candys, Cukren and Nevella – it is found in thousands of diet products. Acesulfame potassium, another non-caloric sweetener, is 200 times as sweet as table sugar. It is approved for use in the United States and the European Union. Neotame, an artificial sweetener made by NutraSweet, is 7,000 to 13,000

Sugar substitutes sold in an American supermarket.

times sweeter than table sugar. The FDA approved it for use in the U.S. in 2002, but it has not yet come to be widely used. Little evidence has surfaced about negative short-term effects of approved artificial sweeteners; the long-term health risks, if any, remain under debate.

Empty Calories

The term 'empty calories', meaning calories derived from foods with few or no nutrients other than carbohydrates or fat, was first employed during the 1950s. At the top of the empty calorie food chart are sugary foods and drinks such as candy, cookies, cakes, pies, ice cream, breakfast cereals and sodas.

John Yudkin, who established the nutrition department at the University of London in 1953, was convinced that there was a clear connection between sugar consumption and many chronic diseases. By the end of the 1950s, Yudkin was campaigning for the elimination of sugar from the diet to prevent coronary heart disease and aid in weight loss. In 1958, he published a diet manual, *The Slimming Business* (1958), which advocated a very low-carbohydrate diet for weight loss. Yudkin published a number of studies supporting his views, which were popular in Britain during the 1960s. In 1972, he published *Pure, White and Deadly: The Problem of Sugar*, a tirade that generated considerable interest among the public in Britain and the United States; still, his views were generally rejected by the medical community, which concluded that dietary fat – not sugar – was the major cause of heart disease.

Medical professionals in the United States concluded that American children consumed too much sugared baby food and sweetened breakfast cereals, resulting in hyperactivity and other health problems throughout their lives. William Duffy, an American journalist and macrobiotic advocate, published the best-selling *Sugar Blues* (1975) about 'the multiple physical and mental miseries caused by human consumption of refined sucrose'. He compared sugar to heroin and called it at least as addictive as nicotine and just as poisonous.

Despite these warnings, Americans continued to increase their per capita sugar consumption, although not all of it was from sucrose. Much of it was from the misnamed high-fructose corn syrup (HFCS). In the 1950s, scientists had learned to refine corn into starch, then convert the starch into glucose, and finally convert the glucose into fructose by adding enzymes. Although it is made from corn, commercial HFCS is chemically similar to sucrose. HFCS contains 45 per cent glucose and 55 per cent fructose, while sucrose contains equal amounts of glucose and fructose. HFCS's advantage was that it was sweeter than sucrose. Its disadvantage was that it was more expensive than sucrose at the time. This changed in the 1970s, when the price of sugar increased in the United States due to quotas and tariffs on imported sugar and subsidies for corn growers which lowered the price for corn. American manufacturers added HFCS to products, particularly beverages. Most subsequent studies have concluded that the human body handles HFCS in the exact same way that it does sucrose. The majority of researchers now conclude that the health issues are associated with the total consumption of refined sugar, not with HFCS.

The term 'junk food', meaning calorie-dense processed foods, particularly sweets, salty snacks and fast foods and sugary beverages that have little nutritional value other than calories, was first used in the 1970s, It was popularized during the following decade by Michael Jacobson, the director of the Center for Science in the Public Interest (CSPI), which from its earliest days has decried high-sugar foods. The problem, according to the CSPI (and many others), is not just eating junk foods, but allowing them to crowd out more nutritious ones.

Refined sugar is an important contributor to excess calorie consumption. According to studies published in 2011 in the prestigious British medical journal *The Lancet*, the global prevalence of obesity has almost doubled since 1980, 'when 4.8 percent of men and 7.9 percent of women were obese. In 2008, 9.8 percent of men and 13.8 percent of women in the world were obese.' An estimated 1.3 billion people worldwide are overweight – half of whom are obese – and the number of people who are overweight is increasing in nearly every country in the world. Excess weight has been linked with high blood pressure, arthritis, infertility, heart disease, stroke, Type 2 diabetes, birth defects, gallbladder disease, gout, impaired immune function, liver disease, osteoarthritis and several types of cancer (including breast, prostate, oesophageal, colorectal, endometrial and kidney cancer).

There are many causes of obesity and overweight, but an examination of research findings led the research institute of the Zurich-based financial firm Credit Suisse to conclude in 2013 that 'While medical research is yet to prove conclusively that sugar is the leading cause of obesity, diabetes type II and metabolic syndrome, the balance of recent medical research studies are coalescing around this conclusion.' They believe that sugar meets 'the criteria for being a potentially addictive substance'. Nowhere is this problem more acute than in the United States, where 61 per cent of Americans are classified as overweight. The annual cost, concludes the Credit Suisse's Research Institute, is also staggering: 30 to 40 per cent of all healthcare expenditures in the United States – about $1 trillion – 'go to help address issues that are closely tied to the excess consumption of sugar', it reports.

Epilogue

Sugar production and consumption remain easy targets for environmental, political and nutrition groups, and for very good reason. Environmentalists hold sugar cane growers responsible for the destruction of rainforests in Brazil, the degradation of the Great Barrier Reef in Australia and the deterioration of the Florida Everglades. Fertilizer and pesticide runoff have caused environmental damage throughout areas where cane or sugar beet are cultivated, including the pollution of fresh and oceanic waters. Contract labourers in sugar-cane-growing areas, such as Haitians in the Dominican Republic, are treated abysmally, and concerns have been raised about migrant workers employed in cane fields in many other countries, including the United States.

Citizens' groups have charged large agricultural interests and food corporations with lobbying for subsidies for domestic sugar production, and high tariffs and low quotas for imported sugar, such as those currently in place in the EU and the U.S. These actions have lowered the price of sugar worldwide, causing severe economic crises in some of the world's least developed countries, and have pushed up the cost of sugar-containing processed foods in developed countries.

Health professionals and nutrition experts have identified added sugar as a major cause of obesity and have pegged it as a contributing factor in many illnesses, including diabetes, heart disease, obesity, peptic ulcers and other chronic diseases. Critics blame large food corporations for lacing their products with excessive amounts of sugar, and for targeting children in their advertising campaigns on television, radio and the Internet, and at or near schools and sporting events.

Because of the criticism, some food companies have begun to decrease the amount of sugar in their foods. Since 2007 the Kellogg Company and General Mills, which produced six of the ten unhealthiest cereals, and did the most child-focused marketing of any cereal company, have lowered the sugar content of the cereals they market to children.

Despite the anti-sugar movement, sucrose remains one of the world's most important foods: it is estimated that about 8 per cent of the total calories consumed in the world comes from sugar, although the amount consumed by populations varies greatly. The global average is about 17 teaspoons (70 grams) per day. At the top are Americans, who consume an average 40 teaspoons of sugar per day – 132 lb (60 kg) per year. Close behind are Brazilians, Argentinians, Mexicans and Australians, with 30 teaspoons per person, per day. Indians eat far less, but the Chinese consume the least among the world's largest countries at seven teaspoons per day – about 4 lb (1.8 kg) per year.

Sugar cane and sugar beet remain among the world's most important crops. Although they are grown in many countries, the major production breaks down to relatively few. Brazil is by far the world's largest grower of sugar cane, producing around 28 per cent of the global crop, but about half of it is converted into ethanol. Brazil exports about 25 per cent of the world's total processed raw sugar. India ranks second in production, and together with China and Thailand accounts for about a third of total world sugar production. The remainder is produced by 114 other countries around the world.

Sugar will remain an important part of the human diet. It isn't just our physiological needs, or the successful marketing of junk-food and soda manufacturers, that attract us to sweet foods and beverages. Sweet-tasting foods – candy, cake, chocolate, ice cream and soda – generate good feelings, and serve as small rewards that help us get through the day. They are often associated with good times – holidays and celebrations such as Christmas, Easter, Valentine's Day, Halloween, birthday parties and weddings. Consumed in moderation, sweet foods and beverages will remain an integral part of our lives far into the future.

Recipes

To make a March-pane
—from *Delightes for Ladies* (London, 1611)

Take two pounds of almonds being blanched and dryed in a sieve over the fire, beate them in a stone mortar, and when they bee small, mixe them with two pounds of sugar beeing finely beaten, adding two or three spoonefuls of rose-water, and that will keep your almonds from oiling: when your paste is beaten fine, drive it thin with a rowling pin, and so lay it on a bottom of wafers; then raise up a little edge on the side, and so bake it; then yce [ice] it with rose water and sugar, then put it into the oven againe, and when you see your yce is risen up and drie, then take it out of the oven and garnish it with pretie conceipts, as birdes and beasts being cast out of standing-moldes. Sticke long comfits upright into it, cast bisket and carrowaies in it, and so serve it; you may also print of this march-pane paste in your moldes for banqueting dishes. And of this paste our comfit-makers at this day make their letters, knots, armes, escutcheons, beasts, birds, and other fancies.

Chocolate Cream
—from François Massialot, *Le Cuisinier royal et bourgeois* (Paris, 1693)

Take a Quart of Milk with a quarter of a Pound of Sugar, and boil them together for a quarter of an Hour: Then put one beaten Yolk of an Egg into the Cream, and let it have three or four Walms: Take it off from the Fire, and mix it with some Chocolate, till the Cream has assum'd its colour. Afterwards you may give it three or four Walms more upon the Fire, and having strain'd it through a Sieve, dress it at pleasure.

To make Liquorish Cakes
—from *The Pastry-cook's Vade-mecum; or, a Pocket-companion for Cooks, House-keepers, Country Gentlewomen, &c.* (London, 1705)

Take 12 ounces of Liquorish scraped very thin, then take two pints and a half of Isop Water, one pint and half of Coltsfoot Water, a pint and half of red Rosewater, two good handful of Rosemary flowers, one handful of Maiden-hair, keep all these together three or four days in a stew Pot or Jug that may be close stop'd, shaking them together two or three times a day, then put them all into a Skilet, and set them upon a soft Fire two hours, then strain it into a Silver Bason, put to it a pound of brown Sugar-candy so let it boil till it grow thick enough to beat to a Paste, when you find it grow pretty thick, take a little upon a Spoon, and beat it with a Knife till it be cold, and then you will find whether it be enough, when you take it off the Fire, it must be beaten with a good strength with a Spoon till it be white, then take some fine Sugare searced, and so roul it up in little Cakes, the best way is to keep beating it to the last, or else it will so crackle that it will never role handsomely, half this Receipt is enough to make at a time.

Portugall Cakes
—from Edward Kidder, *Receipts of Pastry for the Use of his Scholars*
(London, np, *c.* 1720)

Put a pd [pound] of fine sugar & a pd of fresh butter 5 eggs & a little beaten mace into a flatt pan beat it up wth yor hands till tis very leight & looks curdling yn put thereto a pd of flower ½ a pd of currants very clean pickt & dryd beat yn together fill yor hart pan & bake ym in a slack oven

You may make seed cakes ye same way only put carraway seeds instead of currants.

Another Christmas Cookey
—from Amelia Simmons, *American Cookery*, 2nd edn (Albany, NY, 1796)

To three pound flour, sprinkle a tea cup of fine powdered coriander seed, rub in one pound of butter, and one and half pound sugar, dissolve three tea spoonfuls of pearlash in a tea cup of milk, kneed all together well, roll three quarters of an inch thick, and cut or stamp into shape and size you please, bake slowly fifteen or twenty minutes; tho' hard and dry at first, if put into an earthern pot, and dry cellar, or damp room, they will be finer, softer and better when six months old.

To Clarify Sugar
—from Hannah Glasse and Maria Wilson, *The Complete Confectioner; or, Housekeeper's Guide* (London, 1800)

In proportion to three pounds of fine, lump, or powder sugar, which you are to put in a skillet or boiler; break into an earthen pan the white of an egg, with near a pint of fresh water, and beat them up all together with a wisk to a white froth; then put the whole into a copper kettle, or pan, and set them on a clear and slow fire; when it begins to boil, do not fail to put a little more water in, and begin to skim it, till you see the scum appears thick on the top, and the sugar becomes pretty clear; that done, to clear it properly, sift it in a wet napkin, or silk sieve, and pass it thus into what vessel you please, till you want to make use of it.

Note. – If the sugar does not appear very fine, you must boil it again before you strain it; otherwise, in boiling it to a height, it will rise over the pan.

German Biscuits

—from William Alexis Jarrin, *The Italian Confectioner* (London, 1829)

Take cloves, cinnamon, corianders, nutmeg, of each a quarter of an ounce, and pound and sift them (or the essence of those spices will answer the same purpose); two ounces of preserved lemon peel, and one pound of sweet almonds cut into fine prawlings [as for pralines]; mix these ingredients with twenty four eggs, and five pounds of sugar, and as much flour as will make it of a malleable paste. Roll it out into squares, lozenges, ovals, or any other shape; when baked put on them an iceing of chocolate &c. to your taste.

Of Boiling the Sugar

—from M. A. Carême, ed. John Porter,
*The Royal Parisian Pastrycook and Confectioner from the
Original of M. A. Carême* (London, 1834)

There are six degrees of boiling the sugar after it is clarified, viz.; –

First Degree. – *Au Lisse.* – The sugar being clarified, put it on the fire, and after boiling a few moments, take a little of it on the top of your fore-finger, which you press against your thumb; when, on separating them immediately, the sugar forms a fine thread hardly visible, but which you can draw out a little, it is a sign that your sugar is boiled *au grand lisse* but if on the contrary it breaks instantly, your sugar is only *au petit lisse*.

Second Degree. – *Au Perle* (to a Pearl or Bead). – Having boiled your sugar a little longer than stated in the preceding degree, again take some between your fingers, which on separating them immediately will cause the sugar to extend like a string. When this string breaks, your sugar is called *au petit perle*, but if it extends from one finger to the other, without breaking, it is a proof that your sugar is boiled *au grand perle*.

The bubbles thrown up by the sugar in the latter case, should, besides, appear on the surface like small close pearls.

Third Degree. – *Au soufflé.* – Continue boiling your sugar, and then dip a skimmer in it which you strike immediately on the pan.

Then blow through the skimmer, and if that causes small bubbles to pass through it, it is a sign that your sugar is boiled *au soufflé*.

Fourth Degree. – *À la Plume* (to a Feather). – Let the sugar boil up again; then dip in the skimmer and shake it hard, in order to get off the sugar, which will immediately separate itself from it, and form a kind of flying flax. This is called *à la grande Plume*.

Fifth Degree. – *Au Cassé* (to a Crack). – After boiling the sugar a little longer, dip the end of your finger first in cold water, and then in the sugar, and immediately after again in cold water, which will cause the sugar to come off your finger. If it then breaks short, it is boiled *au cassé*; but if, on putting between your teeth, it should stick to them, it is only boiled *au petit cassé*.

Sixth Degree. – *Au Caramel*. – When the sugar has been boiled to the 5th degree, it passes rapidly to a caramel; that is, it soon loses its whiteness, and begins to be very lightly coloured, which proves that your sugar is really boiled to a caramel.

Sugar Candy

—from L.-J. Blachette, *A Manual of the Art of Making and Refining Sugar from Beets* (Boston, MA, 1836)

To fulfil, without omission of anything, the task we have imposed on ourselves, it only remains to speak of the processes by means of which they obtain the sugar candy: but this manufacture, constituting, in France, at least, a part of the art of the confectioner, rather than that of the refiner, we shall only point out very summarily the labours by which they make it.

Sugar candy does not differ from sugar in the loaf except in this, that its crystallization instead of being produced by the stirring, must be effected by repose; and also, that it may be done more slowly, in order that the crystals be more regular, we have removed all causes of a too sudden cooling, and maintained the temperature of the place, where it is to a suitable degree for a time long enough. We have seen, on the contrary, that the operation known under the name of clouding in the manufacture of sugar in the loaf, has for its object to break the crystals, and to promote the

cooling by renewing the surfaces. Thus they call regular crystallization, that by which they obtain sugar candy; and confused
crystallization, that of loaf sugar.

The sirup having been clarified and filtered, is taken again
into the reservoir of the clairée and carried into the cauldron, to be
there baked to a suitable point. This is commonly, by the proof of
the breath, weak or strong, according as we wish to obtain crystals
larger or smaller.

We pour the baked sirup into copper basins, nearly hemispher-
ical, the interior of which is perfectly polished. They are from fifteen
to eighteen inches diameter at their edge, and six to eight inches
deep. At about two inches below the edge, they are pierced on each
side with eight or ten very small holes, through which a thread is
passed, which goes from one edge to the other, passing through
each of the holes. They stop these last either with paste, or by past-
ing paper on the outside of the basin, in order that the sirup, shall
not flow through the holes.

The basins thus prepared are filled to an inch nearly above the
threads, and carried immediately into a hot-house, the temperature
of which is so high that the crystallization will not be complete till
the end of six or seven days. After this time they remove the basins
from the hot-house, and draw off the motherwater, that is, the sirup
that remains liquid. They pour a little water in the basins, to wash
the crystals which are spread over their bottoms. This water is put
with the mother-water.

The bottom of the bed then presents a crystalline bed from
six to nine lines thick. The threads which are covered with crystals
have the form of garlands. They reverse the basins on a vase suitable to drain them well; after which they carry them again to the
hot-house, that they may be well warmed. At the end of two or
three days the sugar is dry; they take it from the hot-house, and
remove it from the basins from which it is easily detached. It may
then be put up for sale.

The mother-water enters into the manufacture of loaf sugar,
like the bastards or lumps.

The tints more or less deep which many kinds of sugar candy
exhibit, belong wholly to the purity of the sirup that has been

used in making them. Sirup perfectly pure gives crystals entirely white.

Sometimes also they shade it in different manners by adding suitable coloring substances. It would lead us entirely from our subject to enter into the detail of these operations, which will be found, beside, in all works that treat of the art of the confectioner, into which they enter thoroughly.

Strawberry Ice Cream
—from Eliza Leslie, *Directions for Cookery* (Philadelphia, 1837)

Take two quarts of ripe strawberries; hull them, and put them into a deep dish, strewing among them half a pound of powdered loaf-sugar. Cover them, and let them stand an hour or two. Then mash them through a sieve till you have pressed out all the juice, and stir into it half a pound more of powdered sugar, or enough to make it very sweet, and like a thick syrup. Then mix it by degrees with two quarts of rich cream, beating it in very hard. Put it into a freezer, and proceed as in the foregoing receipt. In two hours, remove it to a mould, or take it out and return it again to the freezer with fresh salt and ice, that it may be frozen a second time. In two hours more, it should be ready to turn out.

Lemonade
—from *Enquire within upon Everything* (London, 1856)

Powdered sugar, four pounds; citric or tartaric acid, one ounce; essence of lemon, two drachms: mix well. Two or three teaspoonfuls make a very sweet and agreeable glass of extemporaneous lemonade.

Food for a Young Infant

—from Sarah J. Hale, *Mrs Hale's New Cook Book: A Practical System for Private Families* (Philadelphia, 1857)

Take of fresh cow's milk one tablespoonful, and mix with two tablespoonfuls of hot water; sweeten with loaf sugar, as much as may be agreeable. This quantity is sufficient for once feeding a new-born infant; and the same quantity may be given every two or three hours, not oftener – till the mother's breast affords the natural nourishment.

To Make Bon-bons

—from Angelina Maria Collins, *The Great Western Cook Book* (New York, 1857)

Have some little tin moulds, oil them neatly; take a quantity of brown sugar syrup, in the state called a blow, which may be known by dipping the skimmer into it and blowing through the holes, when parts of light may be seen; add a few drops of lemon essence. If the bon-bons are prepared white, when the sugar is cooled a little, stir it round the pan till it grains and shines on the surface, then pour it in a funnel; fill the little moulds; when they are hard and cold, take them out and put them in papers. If you wish to have them colored, put on the coloring while hot.

Efferton Taffy

—from [M. W. Ellsworth and F. B. Dickerson], *The Successful Housekeeper* (Harrisburg, PA, 1884)

This is a favorite English confection. To make it take three pounds of the best brown sugar and boil with one and one-half pints of water, until the candy hardens in cold water. Then add one-half pound of sweet-flavored, fresh butter, which will soften the candy. Boil a few minutes until it again hardens and pour it into trays. Flavor with lemon if desired.

Spinning Sugar

—from Juliet Corson, *Miss Corson's Practical American Cookery*
(New York, 1886)

Spun sugar is used to ornament large candied pieces of fruit and nuts, or nougat; for instance, the preceding piece, the chartreuse of oranges, might be covered with spun sugar after it is taken from the mould; or a pyramid formed of macaroons, cemented with white of egg; or any large ornamental combination piece built up of candied nuts, fruit, and macaroons; or such a stand of candy as is shown upon the table in the background of the accompanying engraving. The sirup is boiled to the degree called 'the crack,' and then a very little of it is poured from a spoon moved back and forth over an oiled knife held as shown in the engraving. The motion must be quick and steady; the spun sugar may be made in the long sections shown in the picture, or in shorter lengths; or it may be spun directly over the piece to be ornamented.

Ginger Pop

—from Isabel Gordon Curtis, *The Good Housekeeping Woman's Home Cook Book* (Chicago, IL, 1909)

To two gallons of lukewarm water allow two pounds of white sugar, two lemons, one tablespoon of cream of tartar, a cup of yeast and two ounces of white ginger root, bruised and boiled in a little water to extract the strength. Pour the mixture into a stone jar and let stand in a warm place for twenty-four hours, then bottle. The next day it will be ready to 'pop.'

Select Bibliography

Abbott, Elizabeth, *Sugar: A Bittersweet History* (Toronto, 2008)

Abrahamson, E. M., and A. W. Pezet, *Body, Mind, and Sugar* (New York, 1951)

Appleton, Nancy, and G. N. Jacobs, *Suicide by Sugar: A Startling Look at Our #1 National Addiction* (Garden City Park, NY, 2009)

Aronson, Marc, and Marina Budhos, *Sugar Changed the World: A Story of Spice, Magic, Slavery, Freedom, and Science* (Boston, MA, 2010)

Aykroyd, W. R., *Sweet Malefactor: Sugar, Slavery and Human Society* (London, 1967)

Barnett-Rhodes, Amanda, 'Sugar Coated Ads and High Calorie Dreams: The Impact of Junk Food Ads on Brand Recognition of Preschool Children', Master's thesis, University of Vermont, 2002

Carr, David, *Candymaking in Canada: The History and Business of Canada's Confectionery Industry* (Toronto, 2003)

Chen, Joanne, *The Taste of Sweet: Our Complicated Love Affair with Our Favorite Treats* (New York, 2008)

De la Peña, Carolyn, *Empty Pleasures: The Story of Artificial Sweeteners from Saccharin to Splenda* (Chapel Hill, NC, 2010)

Deerr, Noel, *The History of Sugar*, 2 vols (London, 1949)

Dibb, Sue, *A Spoonful of Sugar: Television Food Advertising Aimed at Children: An International Comparative Study* (London, 1996)

Duffy, William, *Sugar Blues* (New York, 1975)

Ebert, Christopher, *Between Empires: Brazilian Sugar in the Early Atlantic Economy, 1550–1630* (Leiden and Boston, MA, 2008)

Fraginals, Manuel Moreno, *The Sugar Mill: The Socioeconomic Complex of Sugar in Cuba, 1760–1860* (New York, 1976)

Galloway, J. H., *The Sugar Cane Industry: An Historical Geography from its Origins to 1914* (New York, 1989)

Gillespie, David, *Sweet Poison: Why Sugar is Making Us Fat* (Surry Hills, NSW, 2008)

Hollander, Gail M., *Raising Cane in the 'Glades: The Global Sugar Trade and the Transformation of Florida* (Chicago, IL, 2008)

Hopkins, Kate, *Sweet Tooth: The Bittersweet History of Candy* (New York, 2012)

Jacobson, Michael F., *Liquid Candy: How Soft Drinks are Harming Americans' Health* (Washington, DC, 2005)

Kawash, Samira, *Candy: A Century of Panic and Pleasure* (New York, 2013)

Keating, Giles, and Stefano Natella, *Sugar: Consumption at a Crossroads* (Zurich, 2013)

Kimmerle, Beth, *Candy: The Sweet History* (Portland, OR, 2003)

Krondl, Michael, *Sweet Invention: A History of Dessert* (Chicago, IL, 2011)

Lustig, Robert H., *Fat Chance: Beating the Odds Against Sugar, Processed Food, Obesity, and Disease* (New York, 2013)

Macinnis, Peter, *Bittersweet: The Story of Sugar* (Crows Nest, NSW, 2002)

Mason, Laura, *Sweets and Sweet Shops* (Haverfordwest, Pembrokeshire, 1999)

—, *Sugar-plums and Sherbet: The Prehistory of Sweets* (Totnes, 1998)

Mazumdar, Sucheta, *Sugar and Society in China: Peasants, Technology and the World Market* (Cambridge, MA, 1998)

Mintz, Sidney W., *Sweetness and Power: The Place of Sugar in Modern History* (New York, 1985)

Moreno Fraginals, Manuel, *El Ingenio* (Barcelona, 2001)

Moss, Michael, *Salt Sugar Fat: How the Food Giants Hooked Us* (New York, 2013)

O'Connell, Sanjida, *Sugar: The Grass that Changed the World* (London, 2004)

Osborn, Robert F., *Valiant Harvest: The Founding of the South African Sugar Industry, 1848–1926* (Durban, 1964)

Parke, Matthew, *The Sugar Barons: Family, Corruption, Empire, and War in the West Indies* (London, 2011)

Penfold, Steve, *The Donut: A Canadian History* (Toronto, 2008)

Richardson, Tim, *Sweets: A History of Candy* (New York, 2002)

Scarano, Francisco A., *Sugar and Slavery in Puerto Rico: The Plantation Economy of Ponce, 1800–1850* (Madison, WI, 1984)

Schwarz, Friedhelm, *Nestlé: The Secrets of Food, Trust, and Globalization*, trans. Maya Anyas (Toronto, 2002)

Schwartz, Stuart B., ed., *Tropical Babylons: Sugar and the Making of the Atlantic World, 1450–1680* (Chapel Hill, NC, 2004)

Siler, Julia Flynn, *Lost Kingdom: Hawaii's Last Queen, the Sugar Kings and America's First Imperial Adventure* (New York, 2012)

Strong, L.A.G., *The Story of Sugar* (London, 1954)

Warner, Deborah Jean, *Sweet Stuff: An American History of Sweeteners from Sugar to Sucralose* (Washington, DC, 2011)

Woloson, Wendy A., *Refined Tastes: Sugar, Confectionery and Consumption in Nineteenth-century America* (Baltimore, MD, 2002)

Yudkin, John, *Pure, White and Deadly* (New York, 2013)

—, *Sweet and Dangerous: The New Facts about the Sugar You Eat as a Cause of Heart Disease, Diabetes, and Other Killers* (New York, 1972)

Websites and Associations

Sugar Millers, Refiners, Associations, Organizations and Societies

American Crystal Sugar Company
www.crystalsugar.com

American Sugar Alliance
www.sugaralliance.org

Australian Sugar Milling Council
www.asmc.com.au

Brazilian Sugarcane Industry Association (UNICA)
http://english.unica.com.br

British Society of Sugar Technologists
www.sucrose.com/bsst

China Sugar Association (CSA)
www.csa.gov.cn/outline.asp

The International Society of Sugar Cane Technologists
www.issct.org

The International Sugar Organization
www.isosugar.org

South African Sugar Association (SASA)
www.sasa.org.za

The Sugar Association
www.sugar.org/about-us

Sugar Association of London and Refined Sugar Association
www.sugarassociation.co.uk

SugarCane.Org
www.sugarcane.org

Sugar Producer
www.sugarproducer.com

Tate & Lyle
www.tateandlyle.com

World Sugar Research Organisation
www.wsro.org

High Fructose Corn Syrup

Corn Refiners Association
www.corn.org

High Fructose Corn Syrup
www.sweetsurprise.com

Candy Companies

Cadbury
www.cadbury.co.uk

Hershey
www.hersheys.com

Mars
www.mars.com

Nestlé
www.nestle.com

Perfetti Van Melle
www.perfettivanmelle.com

Beverage Companies

Coca-Cola Company
www.coca-colacompany.com

PepsiCo
www.pepsico.com

Red Bull
www.redbull.com

Schweppes
www.schweppes.com

Sugar Research and Institutes

eRcane (Energie Reunionaise Cane)
www.ercane.re

Mauritius Sugar Industry Research Institute (MSIRI)
www.msiri.mu

Ponni Sugars (Erode)
www.ponnisugars.com

Sugar Processing Research Institute
www.spriinc.org

United States Department of Agriculture –
Sugarbeet Research Unit
www.ars.usda.gov

Vasantdada Sugar Institute
www.vsisugar.com

Photo Acknowledgements

The author and the publishers wish to express their thanks to the below sources of illustrative material and/or permission to reproduce it.

Alamy: p. 106 top (Cindy Hopkins); Bigstock: pp. 6–7 (luiz rocha); The British Library, London: pp. 28, 40, 50; ChildofMidnight: p. 116; Brandon Dilbeck: p. 95; Thomas Dohrendorf: p. 75; Courtesy of Kelly Fitzsimmons: pp. 9, 16, 17, 26, 27, 33, 35, 41, 42, 45, 46, 47, 48, 49 (top), 54, 60, 61, 89, 90, 102, 105, 111, 113, 130; Getty Images: p. 100; Glane23: p. 8; iStockphoto: p. 109 (JenD); Library of Congress, Washington, DC: pp. 22, 36, 53, 49 bottom, 57, 58, 76, 82, 129; Shutterstock: pp. 103, 104 (Roman Samokhin), 106 bottom (ValeStock); Stratford490: p. 92; Tup Wanders: p. 88; Wellcome Library, London: pp. 62, 63, 126.

Index

italic numbers refer to illustrations; **bold** to recipes